I0448102

TIMELESS
WRITINGS
#27

A COMPILATION
FOR MANY WRITERS

TATAY JOBO ELIZES
COMPILER, OCTOBER 2016

Published: October 2016

Self-Publisher/Compiler/Printer

Tatay Jobo Elizes, *born 1934 in Manila, now senior ctizen in Brooklyn, NY. Besides self-publishing, he is busy in piglets dispersal programs for livelihood projects in the Philippines.*

.

Acknowledgement

Gratitude and *acknowledgment belongs to all contributing writers who gave their permission to compile all articles in a book like this to record history based on timely events that directly or indirectly affect our lives. Copyrights of each article belong to the particular author and he/she is free to re-publish anywhere, without any restriction.*

Dedication

I dedicate this book to **all Filipinos** *all over the world and to my immediate family, friends and relatives.*

This book has the following ISBN numbers:
ISBN-13: 978 - 1539394365
& ISBN-10: 1539394360

Disclaimer:

Views are expressed *by the authors alone. Tatay Jobo Elizes does not knowingly publish false information or commit copyright infringement having been given explicit permission to publish this book. Tatay Jobo Elizes may not be held liable for the views of the author exercising his/her right to free expression.*

Free pdf file

FREE reading *as ebook is available to interested parties. Just email me at* **job_elizes@yahoo.com.**

Booklist Websites
http://tinyurl.com/mj76ccq
www.jobelizes6.wix.com/mysit

Contents

1.

Toto Pesing - Alive with our love and prayers

Julia Carreon-Lagoc

Dateline, Sep 30, 2016,
Worldwide-Filipino-Alliance@yahoogroups.com

Dear WFA friends,

Internet is poor in my tiny spot in PH. Luckily, I was able to meet the deadline, and had this column printed in my usual Monday slot. You may like to read on: A phone call can be most devastating. Or unbelievably astonishing — a clarion call about your lottery win! By a stroke of Lady Luck, you are now in the highest rung of the economic ladder in the company of billionaires. Hello Bill Gates! Hi Warren Buffet! How are you, fellow billionaires? We can all play with our wildest imagination, and it's just that: a play.

Oh, well, I can't help being playful, warding off the distressing call. Sunday, Sept. 18, the telephone rang, then voices from the other side of the world—tearfully but audibly—spilled the news:Toto Pesing is dead. Tears just flowed freely and sobs emanated uncontrollably. Unlike my sisters Lolita and Bebita, I wasn't there to cheer or care for my brother in his remaining days on earth.

What epitaph shall we write, I wonder. How about this: Simplicio Rivera Carreon, Jr., NPA. February 3, 1939 –September 18, 2016. Plain and simple. Dates of birth and death. But NPA?

Full disclosure: Toto Pesing, as we lovingly call him, was a member of the New People's Army. Yes, a U-G for a number of years, which means underground, if you're not at home in the jargon of activism. After his stint (word intended for humor) in the Marcosian stockade, the peak of Mt. Madia-as was not an impossible dream. Those were the days when—aware of the uncertainties and fragility of life—our parents would brave themselves for news about their son, Simplicio Jr.: Dead or Alive. Or perhaps, even partially dead or partially alive. Those were exciting times.

I think it was in Pure Foods where he deserted employment, and joined his friends to topple the existing regime. My image of him before he made a sharp detour to the less traveled road—his irrevocable choice—was that of a gentle fellow in the sterling summer of life — hale and hearty, single and fit.

When our father, Simplicio Sr., presented him to us, after Toto Pesing's years of being a U-G, I thought I saw a ghost — thin as thin could be, like an apparition from the grave. Blame, I told myself, to the hide-and-seek life in the Panay hills. Would I be seeing the same frail figure when I go home to

Iloilo this coming Sunday? Ye gods, I'll be seeing him in the casket. A lingering illness in the hospital must have sapped the life in the brother I used to know.

I recall his telling us one time how the kasamas (companions in activism) made him watchdog of the coffers — piles of money and boxes of jewelry for the advancement of the movement. All were dispensed fair and square under his care. Not one tiny bit did he partake for himself, for his wife, and two children. Now his family remains one of the 75,000 claimants under review by the Claims and Reparations Board — indemnification out of the billions stolen by dictator Ferdinand Marcos from the Government Treasury.

Then it was mainstream for Toto Pesing. His health fully recovered, he ran for councilor of the Sangguniang Bayan of our hometown Oton, and winning too. Being away from home most of the time—retired and serving as housekeeper for my daughters' families in the United States—I will surely inquire how Toto Pesing fared as a town official.

Was he ever mindful of the causes he fought for in the mountains of Panay? Being a part of government, what ordinances did he sponsor to alleviate the sufferings of the masses—the disempowered, disenfranchised, dispossessed—whose cause he fought for as a member of the NewPeople's Army?

Then as it is now, the poor—the downtrodden of our countrymen—helplessly await actions. The teeming masses at the base of the social pyramid are enmeshed in the troika of blood, sweat, and tears for sheer existence. Egregious situations remain unchanged: the rich getting richer, the poor getting poorer — the ascending and descending order. Nope, call it disorder — for how long?

It's not goodbye, Toto Pesing. The struggle for social justice must continue. We and the rest of the kasamas pledge to do our part in your honor. With love and prayers, you're alive in our hearts forevermore.

oo0Ooo

2.
Kare-Kare Connection

Julia Carreon-Lagoc

Dateline, Oct 8, 2016 - WFA Group

Nothing ties the Pinoy closest to the homeland than the taste, aroma, and the oh-so-inviting plate of native cuisine. Thoughts of kare-kare compete with the hugs of dear ones, some of whom we haven't seen for years. Savory dishes make up for this retiree's "d-h" job in my daughters' abodes in the U.S. of A., the push-button gadgets notwithstanding.

Ah, the delight of home savory home intensifies as whiffs of grilled bangus or bangus emanate from the kitchen. The freshly-caught milkfish (the sweet-sounding English equivalent) surfaced with the overflow of Brod Gus and Manang Lita's fishpond. Gee, thanks to the heavy rains that resulted in milkfish galore.

In all the times that I had flown PAL Airlines, only once was bangus served in the meals. It was bangus belly oozing with fat. And so, every mealtime, I would ask the flight attendant if there is bangus in the menu, and always I would get "Sorry" for a reply. Bangus or milkfish is the national fish of the Philippines, and PAL being the flag carrier, it is kind of mandatory for the airline to include bangus in its menu

Over at SEAFDEC (Southeast Asian Fisheries Development Center) where I retired Editor of one newsletter, the standing joke is that

SEAFDEC has not come up with an all-belly milkfish. Nada in its years of experimentation. Just belly without the rest of the body parts? Gosh, fisheries scientist or not, no joking with nature please!

Full disclosure: I was never at home with pots and pans. I never learned to cook. My dear departed Rudy could prepare the tastiest pork-leg concoction that I never could. I had always left the kitchen to the maid because I had to catch up with the SEAFDEC shuttle service to Tigbauan where work awaited. Otherwise, I would have to shell out precious money for the public passenger jeep.

The same demand for my time happened when I was teaching at the University of Iloilo—night time was preparing for the next day's subject matter—on the many aspects of English & American Literature. Approbation came when I was made adviser of the UI Star, the university organ. It was most gratifying to see my former students succeed in various fields as lawyers, judges, teachers, clerks. Not to forget: I marched with my students in demos—shouting "Marcos, Hitler, Diktador, Tuta!" in strong defiance of the repressive regime. Those were volatile times—late '60s to early '70s. And thus, KBL (Kapisanan ng Bagong Lipunan) was sold to the citizenry with democracy thrown to the dogs.

Lest I digress any further, kbl (no apologies to the Marcosian KBL) is a favorite of the palate—kadios, baboy, langka combination. It was just the other day that I savored kbl. Marlon, the household chef, got the kbl trio all fresh from the town market selling organic vegies grown by farmers in the rural barangays of Oton, my beloved hometown. Marlon gives credit to the WVSU (Western Visayas State University) weekend classes for his culinary expertise.

Then there is Daisy, the Antique maiden, regaling us with her home-cooked pinakbet—eggplant, okra, string beans, squash or calabasa—with one minor flaw: the squash was not the gooey ripened kind, but was saved by the diced pork and shrimps thrown in. The pinakbet was a blessing to one satiated by Stateside fast-food-to-go. An added bonus is Daisy's nightingale voice that inspires as she goes about her tasks.

Gastronomic delights to die for are right here in Iloilo—the City of Love, if I remember right the appellation. You get the best kare-kare, the Tagalog dish that has earned nationwide popularity, eaten with the unmatched, sweetened ginisang bago-ong. Of course, there is pinakbet that originated in the Ilocos region which, like the kare-kare, was adopted by the rest of the country. The famous chicken and pork adobo that has gained worldwide fame is a standard bill of fare in restaurants. And the fresh lumpia ubod you can find only in the Philippines—as renowned as Bicolandia's famous pili nut marzipan. (Hey, let therest of the world enjoy their prestigious Hershey's chocolates, etc.) I'll have the incomparable pili nut marzipan anytime of the day.

Let me have my buko juice with the young buko meat, so tender they melt in the mouth. (Woe to the cheap restaurateur in the mall food court who includes hardshavings of coconut to my drink of buko pandan. How they desecrate the famous Philippine buko from The Tree of Life, i.e., the coconut.)

Finally, no more tasteless mango from South America forme. I'll have my fill of the sweet, sweet mangoes of home—the Philippine carabao mango—best eaten peeled, i.e, you peel it yourself and bite, the flesh suffused with its own juice. Did it come from Guimaras, Leon, Guimbal, or Igbaras? Or maybe from our own mango tree, laden with ripe fruits, right in our own backyard.

juliaclagoc@yahoo.com

ooOOoo

3.

Memorandum,
filed in the Supreme Court today, in support of the Petition in G.R. No. 225973 against the burial of Ferdinand Marcos in the Libingan ng mga Bayani.

Dateline, September 2016, circulated in the internet among concerned citizens
Please read, please share.
PRELIMINARY STATEMENT

"The first step in liquidating a people is to erase its memory. Destroy its books, its culture, its history. Then have somebody write new books, manufacture a new culture, invent a new history. Before long the nation will begin to forget what it is and what it was. The world around it will forget even faster...The struggle of man against power is the struggle of memory against forgetting."
– Milan Kundera

When Ferdinand Edralin Marcos was deposed, the power he took from the people returned to them. When we forged the 1987 Constitution in the crucible of the 1986 People Power Revolution, it would mark the beginning of our reclamation of what had been wrested from us during decades of atrocities and deceit. Never again would greed devour liberty, nor impunity destroy humanity. Never again would a plunderer and human rights violator conceal beneath a brittle lie of a so-called new society, a rotting morass of martyrs and patriots and a pillaged national coffer. Never again would a dictator and tyrant force us to kneel before him and call him a hero.

Yet, a mere 30 years after the People Power Revolution, we have come to this absurd turning point in our history. An absurdity highlighted by the fact that there is actually no dispute that Marcos was no hero. The President himself publicly admits it, the Solicitor General concedes it. As admitted by both the Solicitor General and counsel for the Marcos Heirs, this Honorable Court characterized Marcos as a dictator in twenty (20) Decisions and as an authoritarian in eighteen (18). This Honorable Court also found Marcos guilty of amassing ill-gotten wealth in two cases where it directed the forfeiture in favor of the Republic Marcos Swiss deposits in the staggering amount of US$661,545,348.60.

This Honorable Court has described the Marcos' administration as a "well entrenched plundering regime of twenty years" "at whose door the travails of the country are laid and from whom billions of dollars believed to be ill-gotten wealth are sought to be recovered." This Court recognized "the hardships brought about by the plunder of the economy attributed to the Marcoses and their close associates and relatives" and declared that it "cannot ignore the continually increasing burden imposed on the economy by the excessive foreign borrowing during the Marcos regime, which stifles and stagnates development and is one of the root causes of widespread poverty and all its attendant ills."

While there is no dispute that Marcos is not a hero, the President nevertheless ordered the burial of his mortal remains in the Libingan ng mga Bayani—the cemetery for heroes-- so that he, as admitted by the Solicitor General, may honor his campaign promise to the Marcoses. This the President has done without even changing the name of the national shrine.

The Libingan ng mga Bayani is no ordinary cemetery. By its very name and pursuant to the acts and laws that establish it, the Libingan is a national shrine established to honor those whom the nation holds in esteem and reverence. Interment in its "sacred and hallowed" premises bestows a singular honor because it is, undeniably, recognition of the deceased's positive and exceptional contribution to the country. Because it was originally intended as a memorial to the nation's war dead -- those "gallant men who brought honor to the country and died for the sake of freedom and independence"—burial therein has potent symbolic power that burnishes with the patina of heroism the reputations and legacies of the dead who would rest there.

Thus, contrary to what the respondents would have this Court believe, the burial of Marcos at the Libingan is not a bland and neutral act bereft of any symbolic, historical or legal significance. It is not a mere returning to the soil. On the contrary, it is an insidious attempt to revise the historical foundation of our Constitution and discredit the fundamental policies lying at its core – that Marcos was a dictator guilty of horrendous abuses, whose like must never again be allowed to hold power over Filipinos.

Burying Marcos in the heroes' cemetery critically weakens the recognition of his crimes that is institutionalized in our Constitution, laws, and jurisprudence. It diminishes and obfuscates the historical premises on which were purposely anchored significant aspects of our constitutional order. It ignores the laws that recognize his crimes and provide for mechanisms to mitigate the suffering they have caused. It holds in contempt a massive body of jurisprudential law that, over three decades, has powerfully articulated the profound villainy of Marcos and his regime.

There is no mystery as to the intent of the respondent heirs of Marcos behind their present insistence upon their patriarch's burial in the Libingan ng mga Bayani. The burial would be reminiscent of the relentless mythmaking of the martial law years to conceal the true nature of a predatory regime founded upon the suffering and ruined lives of millions of Filipinos. It would provide physical proof that Marcos was after all, a hero, and provide also the premise for a revisionist historical narrative totally emulative of him and the long, difficult years of his rule. No wonder then that the Marcos family had so casually disregarded the wish of Ferdinand himself to be buried beside his mother in Ilocos. The Marcoses understand that symbolic power of the Libingan and its strategic value to the national forgetting they so ardently desire.

Petitioners' argument against the Marcos burial is simple: The President's discretion in the matter of the Marcos burial in the Libingan ng mga

Bayani is not absolute. It is limited and bound by the act of the sovereign people during the 1986 People Power Revolution, by the 1987 Constitution produced by that Revolution, by several laws such as Presidential Decree No. 105, Republic Act No. 10368 (also known as the "Human Rights Victims Reparation and Recognition Act 2013") and the international human rights laws codified therein, by Republic Act No. 10086 that mandated that the National Historical Commission of the Philippines as "the primary government agency responsible for history and has the authority to determine all factual matters relating to official Philippine history", by Section 14, Book III of the Revised Administrative Code, and also by the consistent rulings of this Honorable Court memorializing the sins of Marcos and his regime against the Filipino People. Since Presidential power is not untrammeled but subject to the said conditions and limitations, the Honorable Court can exercise its expanded judicial power to fulfill its constitutional role to check grave abuse of discretion and protect the Constitution.

It should be noted that the State accepted the fact of limited Presidential discretion when the Solicitor General himself identified Section 14, Book III of the Administrative Code of 1987 as legal basis for the President's directive to bury Marcos in the Libingan ng mga Bayani. Section 14 clearly requires that the presidential reservation of public land must be for a specific public purpose. The Solicitor General further cited Manosca vs. CA, and City of Manila vs. Chinese Community of Manila, to argue that the recognition of "a person's contribution to Philippine history or culture" constitutes legitimate public purpose that would justify the setting aside of public land under Sec. 14.

By this standard alone, however, it is crystal clear that the burial of Marcos in the Libingan ng mga Bayani does NOT serve any legitimate public purpose. Most certainly, Marcos had no contribution to Philippine history and culture that is worthy of recognition. On the contrary, the tyranny of Marcos, his rapacity, and the violence he systematically unleashed against the people, are matters of fact, established and long-settled and embodied in our Constitution, laws, and jurisprudence.

Remarkably, it is the Solicitor General's own admissions found in paragraphs 203-205 of his Consolidated Comment that provides final and compelling proof that the late dictator had absolutely no contribution to Philippine history and culture worthy of recognition:

"203. Besides, the chapter of Philippine history on Martial Law is not written in ordinary ink. Rather, its every word is written in the blood and tears of recognized and unsung heroes; its every page is a Shroud that has their bloodied but valiant faces on it; and each turn of these pages echoes their cries for freedom.

204. The world has read and heard all of these. In this Information Age, the country's history under the hands of former President Marcos is available at one's fingertips.

205. The point here is simple: the interment of former President Marcos at the Libingan is not tantamount to a consecration of his mortal remains or his image for that matter. No amount of heartfelt

eulogy, gun salutes, holy anointment, and elaborate procession and rituals can transmogrify the dark pages of history during Martial Law. As it is written now, Philippine history is on the side of Petitioners and everybody who fought and died for democracy."

Because this history is enshrined in the Constitution, our laws, and jurisprudence, it is not only subject to judicial notice under the Rules of Court, it binds the State itself, the great powers within it, and each and every government office, agency, and instrumentality.

By actively expediting the burial of Marcos at the Libingan ng mga Bayani, without changing the name of the national shrine that was adopted through Presidential Proclamation, however, the Public Respondents appear intent on ignoring this history and the laws of the land that enshrine it, waiving the conditions imposed upon the Marcos family for the return of his remains, and violating the very Constitution that should rule us all. Verily, by every relevant measure, Public Respondents are guilty of grave abuse of discretion.

Should the Honorable Court, the very institution bestowed by our Constitution with expanded judicial power to enable it to be 'guardian of the Constitution, protector of the people's rights and freedoms, arid repository of the nation's guarantees against tyranny, despotism and dictatorship' , allow itself to be a party to this dismembering and distortion of the history that is embodied in our Constitution, laws, and jurisprudence?

The Petitioners come before the Supreme Court and plead, with utmost respect but also with utmost earnestness: Discharge your duty as protector of the Constitution. Do not let this pass.

(Posted by Concerned Citizens in Aid of the Petition)

ooOOoo

4.

Rejoinder to Danny Gil's Article on Duterte Style,

(included in Timeless Writings-25)

Bernarditas Muller
(Member of UPLakbay & Danny Gil's Friend)

Date: Dateline, September 19, 2016

Dear Danny (Gil),

I share your points below about our new President. I did not know about him and did not vote for him, but only read some articles about what he did for Davao.

I just spent some time in the Philippines, as you know, and talked to friends, relatives, and to all sorts of people I met: drivers, salesgirls, my masahista, helpers, ...What I found out was that while opinions might differ among the "educated, elite" class, the "ordinary" people invariably approve of what Duterte is doing. They feel safer in their communities, even when they go home late at night, they feel safer for their children, they find that the general environment is better for them.

I also thought that now, perhaps, one could think of living out of gated communities and feel safe, unlike the mother of my former secretary, who was brutally murdered by drug-crazed individuals, nor the mother of a colleague (Ambassador) whose mother met the same fate, and others that one read about previously. Did the UN care about their human rights? I also read occasionally here in Europe about drug-related vendetta killings among the youth, but does anybody condemn them about it? The same thing was done in Thailand, even worse perhaps, but did they get world-wide condemnation?

By the way, Thailand started taking off economically also when they undertook serious birth control measures, and distributing condoms freely. I went to dinner at a restaurant dedicated to the success of their condom campaigns- lovely decorations made of those colorful items. I went there with members of the Filipino community in Thailand, and had a lovely dinner. It is a very popular restaurant.

I already told you that, as one who has been dealing with climate change for most of my professional (as a career diplomat) life, and even after my retirement, I agree with everything that Duterte says about it. Not the way he says it (although sometimes one feels like saying that during negotiations!), and the procedures are a little bit more complex than he seems to suggest. For one, the Philippines is certainly not obliged to ratify something it has signed. The US is signatory to the Kyoto Protocol, but did not submit it for ratification. And why should we blindly sign away our rights in an Agreement that is tailor-made to serve US interests, that burdens us with more responsibilities for a problem that we did not cause? We are part of the only legal regime on climate change right now, anyway, so we are more than doing our fair share of addressing climate change, and especially it adverse effects. Our scientists tell us that things are going to get worse, even if the whole world ceases all emissions right now.

But there is one thing that I would like to add to your list, and that is something I know a little about: that finally we have a President who is clearly in favor of an independent foreign policy, one that is focused on national interest, not beholden to some developed country, in particular the United States. The Philippines has not really had one since... maybe the time of Heneral Luna or the massacres during the Philippine-American war? It was considered a courageous act of "independence" when we proclaimed 12 June as our Independence Day, and not the 4th of July! We were taken over from Spain (some thought they were coming as liberators, not knowing that we were part of the booty of the war in Cuba at that time).

The US needed a naval base in the Pacific, but disguised their occupation as "manifest destiny", coming to civilize us who were part of two big Hindu kingdoms since the 12th or 13th century! And then they left hurriedly decades later, not because we were such great negotiators for our sovereignty, but mainly because of a natural phenomenon, the eruption of Mount Pinatubo. We still do not know how much pollution was done to the water tables around Subic and Clark, from where they conducted their bombing campaigns, including the spread of agent Orange, in the Vietnam and also the "secret" war in Laos where they dispersed bombs and mines that even now are still maiming and killing the Laotians (and also the Cambodians, by the way).

The US, and also some former colonial masters from Europe, treat us like some kind of vassal, act like they own the country, and conduct themselves in ways that they would never allow us to do in their own countries. Our famed hospitality is often taken for subservience. Of course, there was corruption under Marcos, and even later, but corruption has two sides: the corrupter and the corrupted. So much is still going on in the Philippines, in terms of environment in particular, perhaps not so much corruption alone but exploitation. With local complicity, naturally. You know the case of the black sand, or magnetite mining that took place in Tanjay, Danny, but it is also taking place elsewhere in the Philippines. Mining is the worse form of exploitation, because it is literally taking away your territory and leaving damage behind. Lots more in terms of biopiracy, sending obsolescent material as "aid" because of the lack of landfills for disposal in their countries, and we allow it, food aid which in fact is all genetically-modified food, etc... Maybe this time, we would not allow these anymore? Much more needs to be done.

One points to economic gains in the country (we are threatened by investors' being frightened by the drug "war" in the Philippines), but does the Economist, which is supposed to know better, state that it has not trickled down to the poor Filipinos? Aah, but that will take time, it seems. Or that our main source of foreign currency is the money from the sweat and blood of our migrant workers? For which, by the way, we are being brought to the UN human rights commissions to respond to charges brought by our own people. I have seen the downside of the migrant phenomenon, the damage done to our society, and yes, even its contribution to the rise of the drug problem among the youth left on their own without proper parental care.

But why this unfavorable press reports especially from the foreign media? Because for the first time, the Philippines has a President who in not a lackey, a "tuta", and that is new to them. I read all the Philippine papers during my stay in Manila, and except for one or two, they just repeated, daily, all the slurs and foul language that was used by the President, as if he was saying these all the time, every day. Heavens, the US President cancelled the meeting with Duterte (gasp!), when all our newly-elected Presidents ran to the US the first time they get, invited or not? He will not meet with another US lackey, the UN Secretary-General, soon to be replaced- how dare he? And to my mind, why should he?

Bernie M.

oo0Ooo

5.

Crimes Vs. Humanity Everyone's Concern

Sen. Rene Sagisag

(Rene Saguisag was born on August 14, 1939 in <u>Mauban, Quezon</u>, Philippines. Saguisag attended elementary school at Makati Elementary School in 1951 He graduated from <u>Rizal High School</u> in 1955 Saguisag went on to graduate with a <u>Bachelor of Arts</u> degree in 1959 from <u>San Beda College</u>. He also later graduated <u>cum laude</u> from San Beda College with a <u>bachelor of laws</u> degree in 1963 and placed 6th in the same year's <u>Bar Examinations</u>. Saguisag also obtained his Master of Laws degree from <u>Harvard University</u> in 1968. Rene Saguisag practiced <u>law</u> as a prominent <u>human rights</u> <u>lawyer</u> in the Philippines from 1972 to 1986. He also became a spokesman for then president elect <u>Corazon Aquino</u> beginning on January 22, 1986. Saguisag was first elected to the <u>Senate of the Philippines</u> in 1987 He remained in the Senate until 1992. As a Senator, Saguisag served as chairman of the committee on <u>ethics</u> and <u>privileges</u>.)

Dateline, Sep 29, 2016, Manila Times
Opinion & WFA Group

All that PNP Top Gun Bato de la Rosa & Co. had to do was use the Internet to find out the drug situation in Colombia. No need to junket to verify whether the hardline bloody policy has failed there (and indeed, all over, such as in Thailand). He would have seen that Colombia Prez Juan Manuel Santos agonizes in explaining to a peasant why he is being prosecuted for planting marijuana whose use is legal elsewhere. Too much blood has been spilled in vain, it seems to me.

Maybe Foreign Affairs Secretary Jun Yasay has not heard of the UNIVERSAL Declaration of Human Rights (UNDR)? A predecessor, Carlos P. Romulo had a hand in its formulation. Jun has asked the world to let and leave us alone on allegations of UNDR violations. And Prez Digs Duterte, Justice Sec Vit Aguirre and Sen. Manny Pacquiao may have no right, in my view, to sniff and condemn some of us as subhumans and therefore cannot have human rights? Bizarre. An apology cannot really undo the damage done by rashness.

The Prez should not apologize for mistakenly identifying an alleged criminal but for naming and shaming anyone at all in gross violation of due process and the presumption of innocence. Those he does not apologize to, tepok na: which investigating prosecutor and judge would shame him?*

Digs has dug up history. But, not deep enough, with all due respect. He may need to dig deeper as a would-be history buff. Now, he even blames God. Did he really attend Ateneo and San Beda?

Anyway, any clan reunion such as we had last Sunday for primo Benedictine Fr. Manuel Maramba, who turned 80, with HILARION Maramba-Henares present, is bound to be HILARIOUS, given his penchant for his last few millions words, if handed a mic. My eldest brod, Tony, would tell me about him in the late 50's, on TV. Kuya Tony idolized him and iconic Claro M. Recto more so.

I first heard Cuya Larry in some college (St. Paul?) program when I was in San Beda. Late 50's. Riveting, I thought. Last we talked at length was a few years ago, when he regaled me with tales of what he would do to quiet his raging hormones. He's going on 93; other members of our Thundering Herd would tell me Cuya Larry is a libido legend, but only in his own mind. Last Sunday, he said he could tell Kamandag Manong Johnny Enrile "di ka nagiisa." Cuya Larry's Fables?

I don't know if he is anti-American but Cuya Larry and Manong have eloquently expressed faith in the Filipino. Pro-Pinoy, no question.

Another kin came over during the party and whispered that the Supreme Court would decide the Libingan ng Mga Bayani (LMB) case 10-5 in favor of the Non-Bayani. Tingnan natin kung ang kamaganak ko ay hindi bulaang propeta. I don't predict as we have up to this week to file our memoranda. I filed a brief paper last Tuesday for Rene, Sr. (me), Rene, Jr. and Rene III stating that the time had not yet come. Better to focus first on Rep. Harry Roque's bill to rename LMB to Libingan ng Mga Bayani at Pangulo. Lincoln is buried in Illinois but remains highly regarded all over the world for RESPECTING everyone. Great Golfer Arnie Palmer, also gone, but is fondly remembered for RESPECTING everyone. Who is fond of DISRESPECTING?

Anyway, safer to talk about the past. As long as Digong revives memories of the Massacres of Bud Dajo and Balangiga (its Bells I saw in Fort Warren just outside of Cheyenne in 1993; PNoy could have asked for their return, before signing EDCA), we should also recall the Chinese Massacres here of 1603 and 1639.

Digs' cunning Chinese hosts might remind him soon, when he visits China and asks for favors. You never know. To put him on the defensive, they may recount that like the fabled and vilified Jews, anywhere, here, the Chinese largely powered trade, labor, and industry in Spanish colonial economy. In spite of the economic benefits given by the Chinese, Spain viewed them with suspicion, fear, and, like we, Indios, do, or did, even with racial contempt (recall Hitler and Jewry).

Given the growing population of the Chinese, government severely restricted Chinese migration here and their businesses were heavily taxed.

By 1581, Guv-Gen Gonzalo Ronquillo de Penalosa created the Parian, for the Chinese in Manila to reside in, well within the range of Spanish cannons.

It became the business center of Manila. On the belief that gold was abundant here, Mandarins came on May 23, 1603, which convinced the Spaniards that a Chinese invasion was imminent, making them suspicious of those in the Parian. The overt hostility of the Spaniards alarmed the Chinese. With such mutual belligerency on both sides, actual confrontation was inevitable.

The Chinese struck on October 3, 1603, in Tondo and Quiapo. Responding Spanish forces were killed to the last man. The Spaniards called > in the Indios and the Japanese residents. (Indios also helped the U.S. in Bud Dajo.) The Chinese then retreated to San Pablo, where they were eventually overwhelmed by forces led by Cristobal de Axqueta Menchaca.

About 23,000 Chinese were massacred. Years later, Governor General Corcuera forced the Chinese to labor in Calamba, and the subsequent abuses committed by Spanish Bossings sparked the second Chinese rebellion. It began in Calamba on November 19, 1639 and spread to other towns in Laguna. The Alcalde Mayor of Laguna and several Spanish priests were killed, and municipal buildings and churches were burned to the ground. For three months the rebels fought in Laguna until they were driven to the mountains.

In February 1640, the Chinese rebel remnants surrendered to Guv-Gen Corcuera in Pagsanjan. Almost 20,000 had been killed.

What about the Muslims in recent times? On February 7 and 8, 1974, also around 20,000 Muslim, Christian and Chinese civilian residents of Jolo died in the the burning of the central commercial town caused by repeated land, sea and air bombardments by the lethal Marcosian war machine. They were caught in the crossfire in the two-day battle of the AFP soldiers and the fighters of the Moro National Liberation Front (MNLF). It was characterized as, "the worst single atrocity" , which rendered scores of thousands Muslims, Chinese and Christians as homeless refugees. (Mamasapano, 44 heavily-armed attacking government troopers and who cares about the Muslim civilian victims?)

The two-day continued Philippine Navy (PN) battleships bombardments from the sea, and the Philippine Air Force (PAF) jet fighter planes, T-28 `Tora-Tora'; warplanes and helicopter gunships bombardments and machine-gun firing from the sky led to the burning of the central Tulay mosque, Chinese Pun Tai Kung temple and the entire commercial town of Jolo. The foreign press exposed the laughter of defenseless and harmless civilians and the looting and ransacking of the Moro-abandoned houses by our soldiers.

The timid local press, quiet. But, I had known about the carnage in a reunion, of our Rizal Hi Class of '55. A classmate who attended the PMA and finished as No. 3 in his class said he took part in it.

We should not tell Digs what we think of his ancestors, may Intsik, may Muslim. Mabalasik. May dugong Waray pa. Masaya. Singing in After Dark in Davao City past midnight. No wonder.

If we cannot have what we like, we have to like what we have? War could be hellish but if we are to blame the Kanos for Bud Dajo and Balangiga, we must also recall what we did to our own civilian Muslim brothers and sisters.

Digs' hero, Macoy, isn't one to the Muslims and to many, who also matter. Last Monday, Digs inaugurated a 405-MW power plant, funded by a fellow Bedan, Andrew L. Gotianun, Sr., in Mindanao. The Bedan Mafia is all over the place.

Where will the Mafiosis take us? To Paradise? Or where Digs tells fellow Bedan Leila de Lima to go? She is giving as good as she gets. Attagirl. But, I am saddened aren't I?

To lift me up, why not listen to Digs and Lei singing in duet, Something Stupid, of which, for some reason, I am often reminded these days.

More time Digs asks for. Let's give it. He will have enough rope to lead us to heaven, sana po, or hang himself with, huwag po naman sana. Presidential temperament should be higher than parochial or mayoral.

To Lei, what doesn't destroy you can only make you stronger. Don't get mad. Don't get even. Get ahead.

Better, Stronger, Together*.

oo0Ooo

6.

'Strategic Diamond' takes shape in the Pacific

Perry Diaz

Dateline, Sept. 8, 2016, PerryScope

Obama and Modi: Over a cup of coffee.

With the signing of the Logistics Exchange Memorandum of Agreement (LEMOA) between the U.S. and India, U.S. President Barack Obama achieved a key part of his "Pivot to Asia" strategy. Indeed, it is a major accomplishment considering that the U.S. had been negotiating such an agreement for the past 12 years.

And the beauty of it is while it strengthens the foundation of Obama's rebalancing of U.S. forces in the Indo-Asia-Pacific region, it also reinforces Indian Prime Minister Narendra Modi's Act East policy; thus, extending India's reach beyond the Indian Ocean into the Western Pacific. What the U.S. and India have accomplished is create a strategic partnership that would be a counterforce to China's aggressive moves in the East and South China Seas and, eventually, the Indian Ocean.

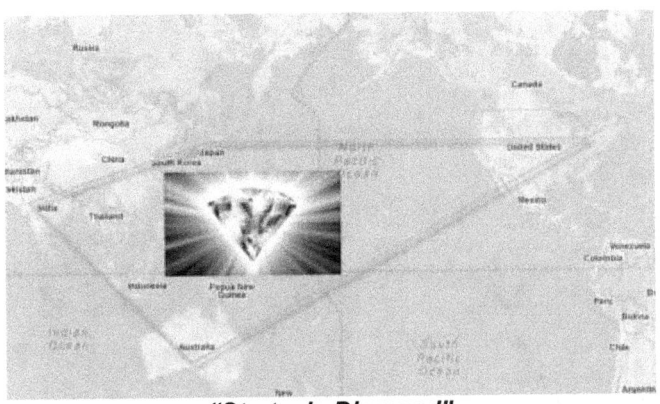

"Strategic Diamond"

In an opinion editorial (op-ed) written by Japanese Prime Minister Shinzo Abe in January 2013, he said that Chinese power is increasingly transfiguring the East and South China Seas into "Lake Beijing." It sounded ominous then. But today, it is pretty close to becoming a reality. China had reclaimed seven reefs in the South China Sea (SCS) and had built artificial islands around them, all within the Exclusive Economic Zone (EEZ) of the Philippines. Recent satellite photos showed that China is building military fortifications including runways, deep-water harbors, lighthouses, and radar installations. And once China declares an Air Defense Identification Zone (ADIZ) over 90% of the SCS that she claims, it would then be nigh impossible to reverse what China did without going to war.

Timetable

Geopolitical and military experts are divided on a timetable. But most of them agree that war between the U.S. and China could happen sooner or later. Some say within a year. Some say 2020, while a few others say 2034.

Evidently, China has put her military modernization plan on the fast tract. While the U.S. still has military advantage, China is fast catching up. And many experts believe that 2020 would be the year when China could surpass the U.S. if the U.S. lets up with her technological edge over China. It is important to note that the Chinese generals have the mindset of Sun Tzu; that is, they wouldn't go to war for as long as they believe the U.S. is stronger than China.

First and Second Island Chains

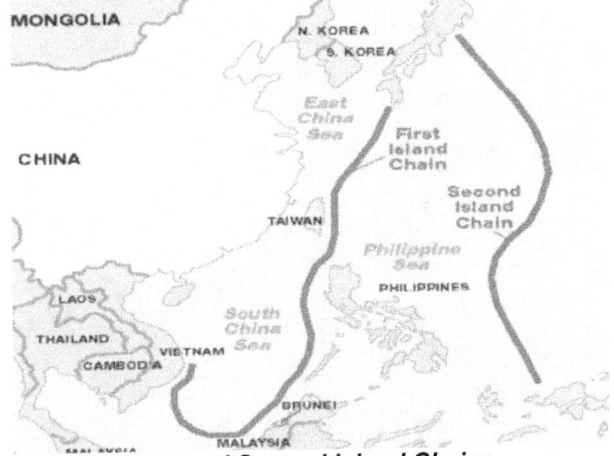

First and Second Island Chains

If you've been following American military strategy since the beginning of the Cold War, she's been busy building military alliance with countries in the Indo-Asia-Pacific region. To date, the U.S. has defense treaties with Japan, South Korea, Taiwan, the Philippines, Thailand, and Australia. These treaty allies – with the exception of the Philippines – are strong militarily, politically, and economically.

While the Philippines may be the weakest link in the First Island Chain – from Japan through Taiwan, the Philippines, Borneo, Malaysia, and Vietnam – it's geostrategic location is a natural barrier against Chinese intrusion into the Second Island Chain –from Japan through Guam, the Marianas Islands, and Papua-New Guinea.

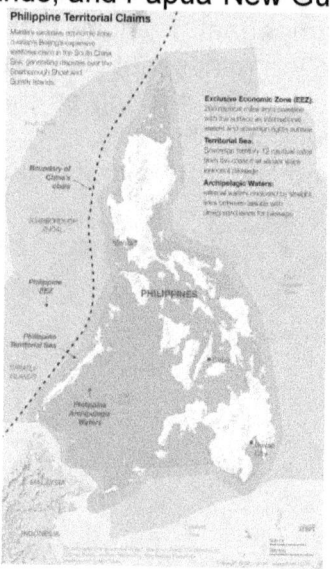

It did not then come as a surprise when the U.S. and the Philippines signed – over the objections of leftists politicians and activists — an Enhanced Defense Cooperation Agreement (EDCA), which is to allow the deployment of American military forces on a "rotational" basis in the country. Right now, four airbases and an army base have been selected to base them. In addition, the U.S. Navy is using the former Subic Bay Naval Base for port calls and to replenish supplies, while American surveillance aircraft are stationed at the former Clark Airbase.

In addition to the six treaty allies, the U.S. has strategic partnership with Singapore, where an American naval flotilla is home ported. The U.S. is also developing defense relationship with Vietnam, while Malaysia and Indonesia aren't too far off the grid. With Malaysia and Indonesia having maritime territorial disputes with China on their own, they welcome the presence of American warships in the SCS. They know that for as long as the U.S. maintains a superior naval presence – more than 200 warships and 400 warplanes deployed to five aircraft carrier strike groups — in the Indo-Asia-Pacific waters, China would be contained.

The question is: How can the U.S. maintain her primacy in the Indo-Asia-Pacific region? The answer is in Prime Minister Abe's op-ed. He said: *"To counteract China's primacy in southern waters [SCS], Japan must augment its combat and police capabilities while forging a 'diamond' with the United States, Australia, and India to defend the commons in East and South Asia."*

Red line

Japanese Prime Minister Shinzo Abe reacts to China's "red line" threat if Japan will join the U.S.-led freedom of navigation operations (FONOPS) in the South China Sea.

The Chinese must have taken note of Abe's op-ed because recently *Kyodo News*reported that China's Ambassador to Japan, Cheng Yonghua, had told a Japanese official that if Japan's Maritime Self-Defense Force joined the U.S.-led freedom of navigation operations (FONOPS) in the SCS, Japan would have crossed a "red line."

In another diplomatic incident, China warned Australia about a media release pertaining to the Permanent Court of Arbitration (PCA) ruling that favored the Philippines. The media release quoted Australian Foreign Minister Julie Bishop as saying: "The Australian Government calls on the Philippines and China to abide by the ruling, which is final and binding on both parties." Immediately, the Chinese protested against Bishop's "wrong remarks."

Meanwhile, Philippine President Rodrigo Duterte sent former President Fidel V. Ramos to Hong Kong to meet up with some contacts in China. While nothing definitive came out of the meetings, the way is paved for Duterte to initiate bilateral talks with China. China agreed. However, she said that the Philippines mustn't bring the PCA ruling to the table, which raises the question: Would China be willing to give some concessions to the Philippines or would she insists on having it all? But the question is not about keeping those little rocks, reefs, and shoals, it's about who would reign over the entire Indo-Asia-Pacific region?

Chinese Dream

Chinese Admiral Liu Huaqing

In 1982, Chinese Admiral Liu Huaqing, the architect of China's modern naval strategy, was quoted as saying that it would be necessary for China to control the First and Second Island Chains by 2010 and 2020, respectively. "The PLA Navy must be ready to challenge US domination over the Western Pacific and the Indian Ocean in 2040. If China is able to dominate the Second Island Chain seven years from now, the East China Sea will become the backyard of the PLA Navy," he said.

However, China is running behind schedule. But if nobody stops her from reclaiming the Scarborough Shoal, she would be in a position to control the First Island Chain by 2020, the Second Island Chain by 2030, and the Indian Ocean by 2050.

Ultimately, it would all come down to who would be the strongest. But if what Abe had envisioned in 2013 would come to fruition, which is to form a strategic partnership among the four Indo-Asia-Pacific maritime democracies – Japan, U.S., Australia and India — the time may not be too far away for them to challenge any attempt by China to assert total control over the region. Indeed, with the signing of LEMOA, the "strategic diamond" is taking shape in the Indo-Asia-Pacific region.

(PerryDiaz@gmail.com)

ooo0ooo

7.

Foreign Policy Fiasco

Perry Diaz
Dateline, September 19, 2016, PerryScope

Philippine President Rodrigo Duterte, in white, walks away with officials following the ASEAN summit plenary meeting at National Convention Center in Vientiane, Laos, Tuesday, Sept. 6, 2016. (AP Photo/Gemunu Amarasinghe)

It was a very strange week! Was it a full moon... or was it sign of the times? Indeed, a nation's leader going ballistic is not the usual norm even with the likes of... well, I don't want to distract you from the issues so let's move on.

The recent brouhaha on the eve of President Rodrigo Duterte's departure for his first foreign foray to the ASEAN Summit in Vientiane, Laos has left many people wondering what was going on in Duterte's mind? Frankly, a national leader uttering the curse *"putang ina"* – "son of a whore" – to the Pope, the United Nations Secretary General or to the President of the United States, is demeaning the position he holds. And worst, it gives a bad image to the people he leads. And yet, 91% of the Filipino people incredibly hold him in high esteem! As George Takei loves to say, *"Oh my!"*

It all began when Obama, before embarking on his last foreign trip, said that he'd talk to Duterte in Laos about human rights violations. Well, "human rights" is something that apparently hit a raw nerve in "Digong" – Duterte's street moniker – who is reputed to condone killings of illegal drug pushers and users because he said they're not "human beings." Which reminds me of what Digong had told a crowd of cheering admirers, saying he doesn't mind being likened to the late Ugandan dictator Idi Amin, whom human rights activists blamed for the deaths of up to 500,000 people in the 1970s.

Digong and Amin

Duterte and the "Last King of Scotland".

And the similarity between Digong and Amin reminds me of the movie, *"The Last King of Scotland,"* where Amin's mercurial temperament and extreme mood change often makes one wonder if Amin had multiple personalities? Indeed, Duterte once told a group of reporters, *"Ako, palabas-masok ako sa bipolar. One moment seryoso ako, one moment tatapunan ko kayo ng biro."* (I am bipolar. I am serious one moment, and the next moment I will joke with you.)

If true – meaning that he's not joking about suffering from bipolar disorder – then we could be in for a roller coaster ride for the six years of his presidency. Indeed, his underlings – cabinet secretaries and department heads – would be scratching their heads (confused) and wiping their sweating armpits (nervous) every time Digong would give conflicting orders. While they are expected to be compliant and subservient, they would follow Digong's orders, as they understood them, which could lead to bureaucratic chaos. The end result would be a dysfunctional government. But running a government gone berserk is one thing; running amuck around international summitries and gatherings is unspeakably horrible, to say the least.

Digong and Obama

It did not then come as a surprise when Digong bad-mouthed Obama, the leader of the world's most powerful country, before he left for Vientiane to attend the ASEAN meeting. When a reporter asked him how he would explain his administration's recent extrajudicial killings to Obama, he said that Obama must respect him and not just throw questions at him. He then blurted,

"*Putang ina*, I will swear at you in that forum!" And when Obama heard about this, all he said was "He's a colorful guy" and cancelled the meeting. Yep, what Duterte did was like a doberman biting the toe nails of an elephant; it didn't hurt the elephant.

But Digong – a fearless street fighter – has the temerity to admit in front of television in Indonesia that he killed a prisoner who raped an Australian missionary when he was mayor of Davao City. Instantly, the limelight was on him. But is that how a national leader should project himself on the international stage?

While it might have awed some of the leaders attending the summit and treated him like a celebrity, Digong's explosive speech on television had left little doubt that he's someone to be shunned and treated as an international pariah.

One-two-three...

U.S. Special Forces in Mindanao.

But what Digong did in Vientiane was just an appetizer for the media whose voracious appetite for sensational and controversial scandals has no end. And no sooner had Digong landed in Manila than he dropped a bombshell on the U.S. Special Forces fighting the terrorists in Mindanao, saying they "have to go." His reason for their eviction was to keep them from being killed by the Abu Sayyaf terrorist group. The next day — like a one-two-three punch — he announced that joint patrols with the U.S. in the South China Sea would end. He also announced that the Philippines would buy arms from China and Russia, saying that deals are already "in the pipeline." He then disclosed that China had offered to provide him with a personal plane to use. His own "Air Force One"?

The following day, Chinese Vice Foreign Minister Liu Zhenmin welcomed Digong's "independent foreign policy" and remarked that relations between the two countries "are at a new turning point." Not so fast, pal, because the following day, Digong declined the offer saying that the plane might have more problems than him taking commercial flights. And jokingly – or seriously? – he said the plane might explode!

That, in a nutshell, was Digong's maiden "independent foreign policy." Evidently, he didn't consult with his Foreign Affairs Secretary Perfecto Yasay Jr. and National Defense Secretary Delfin Lorenzana to make sure that the independent foreign policy he was pursuing would not put the country in harm's way. But while there is nothing wrong with taking an independent course in foreign affairs, history tells us "Never burn your bridges" because you'd never know when you would need it to go back.

Damage control

A few days later, Yasay flew to Washington DC to meet with U.S. Secretary of State John Kerry to clarify that Duterte's message to the U.S. Special Forces was not an indication of policy shift.

He told Kerry, *"We cannot forever be the little brown brothers of America."* Huh? It's amazing that some Filipinos are still using that archaic line.

"We cannot forever be the little brown brothers of America." – Yasay

It must have been excruciatingly painful for Yasay trying to convince Kerry that what looked like a triangle was actually a square. But he didn't realize that Kerry preferred a circle. As someone once said, "Foreign policy is not what it seems." Indeed, what you asked for may not be what you'd get... if you'd get anything at all.

Meanwhile, a few days later, Lorenzana told the House of Representatives' Appropriation Committee that American troops would remain in Mindanao despite the president's statement that he wanted them out of Mindanao. "We still need them there because they have the surveillance capability that our Armed Forces don't have," said Lorenzana, a retired major general. He also told the House committee that the danger of Abu

Sayyaf killing or kidnapping the American troops is remotely possible.

Brink of insignificance

While one might presume that the Department of National Defense is in good hands and standing on solid ground, the Department of Foreign Affairs is on shaky ground led by a person whose foreign affairs experience could be categorized as apprentice. And worst, we have President Duterte who has oversized cojones play-acting as Superman, Batman, Iron Man, and Spiderman all rolled into one.

This is not meant to disparage Duterte and Yasay. But the two personify the Republic of the Philippines in the international stage where world leaders see in them the strengths and weaknesses of the country they represent. All it takes is one major foreign policy fiasco to drive the country to the brink of insignificance.

Today, four decades after Idi Amin fled Uganda into exile, many people still vividly see the image of the brutal dictator lording over his ravaged country, which begs the question: Is the Philippines heading the way of Uganda?

(PerryDiaz@gmail.com)

ooOOoo

8.

China Sets Eyes on Benham Rise

Perry Diaz

Dateline, September 27, 2016, Perry Scope

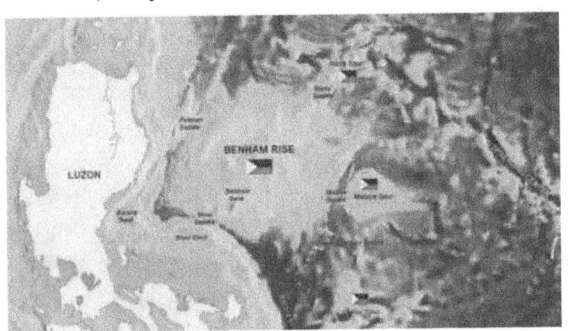

As soon as the United Nations had awarded Benham Rise to the Philippines than China sets her eyes on this undersea landmass in the Philippine Sea. According to the Department of Environment and Natural Resources (DENR), this 13-million-hectare area off the coast of Aurora province is potentially rich in mineral, natural gas deposits, and manganese nodules that are vital in the production of steel. Studies conducted by DENR have also shown large deposits of methane in solid form (methane hydrate or methane ice). Further studies also showed that natural gas deposits in the area would enable the Philippines to achieve energy sufficiency.

The Benham Rise is within the Philippines' exclusive economic zone (EEZ). However, she did not claim it until 2008. The following year, the Philippines, which was the sole claimant, formally submitted her claim to the U. N. Commission on the Limits of the Continental Shelf.

Larger than the entire island of Luzon, Benham Rise was awarded to the Philippines in 2012, after the United Nations approved her claim that Benham Rise was an extension of her continental shelf. In December 2013, the U.N. Convention on the Law of the Sea (UNCLOS) informed the DENR – with finality — that Benham Rise is part of the country's continental shelf and territory. As such, it is not subject to any maritime boundary disputes and claims. Wrong!

In February 2016, the Philippines' Bureau of Fisheries and Aquatic Resources (BFAR) reported that several Chinese ships were seen in the Benham Rise. The following July, China Daily published a report about China's "secret undersea exploration" in the Benham Rise area. The report said that China discovered massive mineral deposits. It also said that the volume of natural gas deposits in the area was at par with what was discovered in the Spratly Islands.

Quid pro quo

Xi Jinping and Rodrigo Duterte (Credit: CNNPH)

With the recent warming up of relations between China and the Philippines under the administration of President Rodrigo Duterte, China has a grand opportunity to solidify her hold on the Spratly Islands and Scarborough Shoal when Duterte visits China in October. It is expected that Chinese President Xi Jinping would shower Duterte – who has shown willingness to put the territorial disputes between the two countries in the back burner – with low-interest loans for infrastructure and economic development projects, and military hardware. But as China had demonstrated in previous *"quid pro quo"* deals with third-world countries, she'd get more than what she bargained for.

Indeed, China's "wish list" could include lucrative economic contracts in the areas of energy, transportation, port management, agriculture, mining, and oil and gas exploration. It wouldn't be surprising if China acquires long-term agreements to use the former American bases – such as the Subic Naval Base and Clark Airbase — as logistical support bases for her growing navy and air force that she needs to project power into the Second Island Chain, which runs from the Ogasawara Islands and Volcano Islands of Japan through Guam and the Marianas to Papua-New Guinea.

If China builds an artificial island on top of Scarborough Shoal (which at 58 square miles is slightly smaller than the area of Quezon City, the capital of the Philippines), she'd be in a position to militarize it. And once militarized – like what she did to the seven artificial islands she built in the Spratlys — she'd be able to control the choke point at the Bashi Channel in the Luzon Strait, which is the gateway to the Philippine Sea… and beyond.

Chinese Dream

Chinese Admiral Liu Hoaqing.

In my column ***"China raises the ante"*** *(July 31, 2013),* I wrote:*"Last June 27, 2013, an intriguing article appeared in the Want China Times titled,***'China to take Second Island Chain by 2020: analyst.'*** It says: 'Within seven years, China will be able to control the Second Island Chain — a series of island groups that runs north to south from the Japanese archipelago to the Bonin and Marshall islands — now that the PLA Navy commands the nation's first aircraft carrier, according to the Hangzhou-based Qianjiang Evening News.'*

"The article also said: 'In 1982, Admiral Liu Huaqing, the former commander of the PLA Navy and the mastermind of China's modern naval strategy, said that it would be necessary for China to control the First and Second Island Chains by 2010 and 2020. The PLA Navy must be ready to challenge US domination over the Western Pacific and the Indian Ocean in 2040. If China is able to dominate the Second Island Chain seven years

from now, the East China Sea will become the backyard of the PLA Navy.' "

Lake Beijing

"Lake Beijing" bounded by Second Island Chain.

With China's goal of controlling the vast Western Pacific, which includes the East China Sea (ECS), South China Sea (SCS), and the Philippine Sea, the entire Western Pacific would be transformed into "Lake Beijing." The Philippines would be right in the middle of the lake, isolated from the rest of the world. "Lake Beijing" would also encompass the mineral-rich Benham Rise as well.

As things are today, China is behind in her timetable to achieve control over the First Island Chain, which includes the ECS and SCS. However, by militarizing the Spratly archipelago, the Paracel Islands, and Scarborough Shoal, China would be able to establish a "strategic triangle" formed by these three island groups where China could monitor – and control – all the movements in the SCS. The next step would be to declare an Air Defense Identification Zone (ADIZ) over the entire SCS. With an ADIZ already in place over the disputed Senkaku Islands in the ECS, China would then be ready to break out into the Second Island

Chain right up to America's doorsteps, Guam. And the last – and final — step would be to take full control of the choke point at the Strait of Malacca, and eventually... penetrate the Indian Ocean.

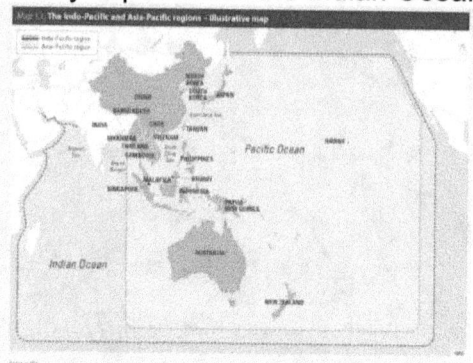

Indo-Asia-Pacific Region.

What is at stake in these disputed waters is control of the huge mineral deposits, marine resources, and the world's busiest maritime lanes. What could the U.S. and her allies in the region do to stop China from gaining control over this huge body of water, which extends more than 10,000 miles from the Indian Ocean to the Second Island Chain?

If the U.S. fails to stop China, she might as well kiss the Indo-Asia-Pacific region goodbye and cocoon herself into isolation just like before she entered World War I. But inaction does not guarantee peace either. The "Munich Appeasement" of 1938 did not stop Germany from invading Czechoslovakia. On the contrary, it emboldened Germany to pursue territorial expansion, thinking that the Great Powers – particularly America — wouldn't intervene. In fact, as Germany continued her conquest of Europe, then U.S. President Franklin Roosevelt told the American people in 1940: "I have said this before, but I shall say it again and again: your boys are not going to be sent into any foreign wars." Wrong!

Iran's Hassan Rouhani, China's Xi Jinping,
and Russia's Vladimir Putin.

When Japan attacked Pearl Harbor on December 7, 1941, Roosevelt declared war on Japan the following day. A few days later, Germany declared war on the U.S; thus, bringing the world to war once again for the second time.

North Korea's Kim Jong Un.

Which begs the question: Is appeasement a guarantee for peace or just a momentary stop-gap that would only encourage a rogue country – China, Russia, North Korea or Iran — to start another world war? Sad to say, if history is the barometer of things to come, the imbroglio in the SCS has all the elements of war in the offing. And

as China sets her eyes on Benham Rise, the world teeters on the brink of World War III.
(PerryDiaz@gmail.com)

oo0Ooo

9.

The Philippines at a dangerous crossroads

Perry Diaz

Dateline, Oct. 3, 2016, PerryScope

President Rodrigo Duterte's ascension to the Philippine presidency happened at a time when the country was anxiously waiting for the Permanent Court of Arbitration's (PCA) ruling on China's maritime claims in the South China Sea (SCS). And when the ruling was finally released on July 12 invalidating China's "nine-dash line" claim and that China had no historical rights to the rocks, reefs, and shoals in the SCS, the newly installed president found himself in the international limelight. And when the media asked him where he stood in regard to the arbitration case his predecessor former President Benigno S. Aquino initiated, Duterte gave conflicting statements. In a matter of days – nay, hours -- Duterte was pushed into the choppy waters of the SCS to deal with China's aggression.

He found himself in a precarious situation with nobody to call for help. It was sink or swim. And when U.S. President Barack Obama offered to meet with him at the ASEAN Summit in Vientiane, Laos to talk about their countries' security relationship and the issue of human rights violations, Duterte was miffed.

He didn't like Obama saying that he'd like to talk to him about human rights violations. But had he known how U.S. foreign policy works, he would have understood that if he expected the American "sugar daddy" to give the Philippines military assistance, his government would have to pass the litmus test for the preservation of human rights. That was just the way the U.S. Congress would allow the U.S. government to give military assistance to other countries. Instead, just like his "kanto boy" upbringing, Duterte responded the way he was used to, saying: " 'Putang ina,' I will swear at you in that forum." "Putang ina" is the Tagalog phrase for "son of a whore."

For Duterte's outburst, Obama cancelled the meeting. Duterte missed an opportunity to solidify his administration's relationship with the country's only treaty ally and benefactor. **Independent foreign policy** Soon after that incident, which by international standards shouldn't have happened, Duterte started talking about pursuing an "independent foreign policy."

He indicated that he'd ask Russia and China to supply the Philippines with military armaments. He said that he'd open the country to trade with Russia and China; and is prepared to give them 120-year leases. And what would he get in return for prostituting the Philippines to these two countries run by dictators? Oh yeah! Duterte might finally get his railroad in Mindanao. But he should know that whatever economic assistance the Philippines gets from China, China is going to get back huge slices of the Philippines' priceless patrimony.

War against drugs With Duterte's takeover of the government, he pursued to eliminate the drug menace, which according to him has created 4,000 drug pushers and addicts... and counting. He encouraged the national police to go after them and to kill them if they resisted arrest.

And it was at this juncture that Obama was alarmed. Guided by the *Leahy Act,* he wanted to discuss with Duterte the more than 3,000 extrajudicial killings since he took office two months ago. Named after Sen. Patrick Leahy, the law's principal sponsor, *Leahy Act* prohibits the U.S. Department of State and Department of Defense from providing military assistance to foreign military units that violate human rights with impunity. **Gone ballistic** And that's when all hell broke loose! Duterte went ballistic and uttered the "P" word, which is the equivalent of the American "F" word. Duterte then issued – through the media -- a series of policies that would severely affect U.S.-Philippine relations.

In a fit of anger, he declared that he would soon "cross his Rubicon" with the U.S. He also said that the U.S.-Philippine joint military exercises that are now happening would be the last during his presidency. He also said that he would terminate the Philippine Navy's participation with the U.S. in joint patrols in the West Philippine Sea. And, worse, he said that the Philippine Navy would not venture beyond the 12-mile territorial limit, which would be tantamount to surrendering the country's 200-mile exclusive economic zone (EEZ) to China.

If this is the gist of his "independent foreign policy," then what we're seeing here is not independence but a capitulation of national sovereignty, which would undoubtedly lead to vassalage under China. I say this because China will not stop bullying the Philippines and other neighboring countries that don't have the ability to defend their sovereignty and territorial integrity. Simply put, China wants the entire SCS for herself. And she's not coy about it.

Deterrence by denial

Honestly, no country in Asia could defend herself against China's aggressive moves. Even Japan, the world's third largest economic power after the U.S. and China, has to ally herself with the U.S. and allows the U.S. to deploy 50,000 troops on her soil, including several naval and air bases. Ditto with South Korea, who is under constant threat from nuclear-capable North Korea. With several U.S. air bases and 28,000 American troops stationed in her territory, South Koreans feel safer knowing that for as long as the American forces are in their country, North Korean dictator Kim Jong Un would think twice before invading South Korea. Before the American bases were kicked out of the Philippines in 1992, their presence served as deterrence against foreign invasion. The purpose of what is known as "deterrence by denial" is to make aggression difficult and unprofitable by rendering the target harder to take, harder to keep, or both.

To achieve this, the defenders – Filipino forces with the aid of American forces stationed in the Philippines – must be able to inflict substantial damage to the invaders.

Salami-slicing

It's interesting to note that two years after the Americans had left, the Chinese took possession of Panganiban (Mischief) Reef and built fortifications on it. In 2012, China grabbed Scarborough Shoal and prohibited Filipino fisherman from entering its huge lagoon to fish. Two years after that, China started building artificial islands on seven reefs and shoals – including the Mischief Reef – in the Spratly archipelago, all within the Philippines' EEZ. Thus far, China's unimpeded salami-slicing of Philippine territory has put into question the Philippines' defense capability or the lack thereof. With Duterte's "independent foreign policy" crafted in an atmosphere devoid of reason, the PCA's ruling, which invalidated China's "nine-dash line," is imperiled and the ruling could be deemed moot and academic in light of Duterte's "retreat" from the SCS.

Indeed, the Philippines is not in a position to sever her relationship with the U.S., which Duterte had indicated in his public pronouncements. But his threats to do so are alarmingly dangerous. It doesn't make any sense why he would kowtow to China and Russia at the expense of the U.S., the country's strongest military ally, biggest foreign investor, and second largest export market next to Japan. Unlike communist China, both the Philippines and the U.S. have compatible democratic institutions and both subscribe to the rule of law and adhere to the norms of international order. China doesn't.

In these troubled times, the Philippines has reached a dangerous crossroads where she has to determine which road to take. While it is tempting to try new and uncharted roads, President Duterte should – nay, must! – take the road that would lead the country to economic prosperity and the preservation of individual freedom for her citizens. And if he takes the wrong turn, it could lead to perdition. (PerryDiaz@gmail.com)

oooOooo

10.

Ominous?

Erick San Juan

Dateline, September 27, 2016

The presidency of Rodrigo Roa Duterte has its many firsts and for some it's too good to be true especially that the country's experiences from the past leaders, the recent ones were all tainted with so much irregularities and anomalies. Filipinos thought that the 'new normal' nowadays are the things that were passed on from previous administrations or could it be that the majority are just too tired and let things be as they are – the status quo.

Although netizens who are aware of the current issues are the ones who are very active in posting their views and comments of the things they strongly disagree or agree via the internet. It is a fact that the last election maximized the use of the internet in reaching out to the electorate.

Now that the 'majority' has voted a strong and brave leader, the rest has to bear with him for the rest of his six-year term or less? If one will notice that in several speeches of President Duterte, he kept on mentioning that "if he can finish his term" or "if he is still alive" to fulfill his promises. The several "ifs" that seem to make him accomplish things in a hurry and in the long run, some empty promises being made.

What is also ominous according to a psychic friend, is his use of DU30. I was reminded that most journalists writes 30 which means death or end.

Desperately wanting to finish such a huge problem like the war on drugs in a short span of time, President Duterte also visited as many military camps as possible when he has the time. Seeking the help of the military arm to fulfill his goal of a drug-free country, he promised a lot of benefits to the men in uniform and their families including a doubled monthly salary, as soon as possible. But he forgot that the government is still tied to the last administration's budget and that the huge problem of rehabilitation of hundreds of drug users/pushers is impossible to achieve and so he is perceived making commitments beyond in the process.

Our president has done this due to his heightened emotion against the drug problems but Mr. President, you have to be very careful in handling your emotions being exposed through your words, no matter how sincere you are, it will only be used against you if you fail. Sadly, most of these words were directed to officials of foreign countries and organizations. Economists and those who are not so fond with President Duterte are now blaming him for the poor performance of our 'economic fundamentals'.

With the hearings in both houses of Congress (in aid of legislation), several matters of great importance were exposed.

In his article at the Manila Times, Atty. Al Vitangcol 3rd wrote his observations – "The recent justice committee hearings in the Senate and House of Representatives revealed and made public a lot of things that were only heard from the grapevine before. Now, these things are officially out and part of the public records, by way of the Minutes of the committee hearings.

One of these disclosures is the alleged Plan B, which is to destabilize the Duterte Administration and create a scenario to oust President Rodrigo Duterte. If this will not work, then impeach President Duterte. If all else fails, then assassinate the President. Once Duterte is gone, install Vice President Leni Robredo as the new President of the Republic.

Senator Alan Peter Cayetano revived talks, this time officially during the Senate Committee on Justice and Human Rights hearing, of the Liberal Party's alleged Plan B to unseat President Duterte.

My insight says otherwise. The supposed Plan B will not prosper and will not muster the support of the people and the military. However, even before Plan B could take off, the groundwork for "Plan D" has already been laid."

And what is this Plan D all about?

Plan D is the full military takeover of the government in the event of President Duterte's sudden departure before 2022. His sudden departure could be the result of any of these things

– impeachment, forced ouster by foreign states, assassination, or natural death.

In his speech before the 9th Infantry Brigade, the President said in part (while showing and waving the third "narco-list"), "How can I handle this? I cannot just arrest them and kill them. That is nothing. I do not like Martial Law. This will destroy your children, or your grandchildren and the next generation. That is why we are ready to die ... because they are not safe anymore."

The President admitted that it is the technicality of the law that makes it hard for him to deal swiftly with the problem of illegal drugs and criminality.

He added, "if that problem outlasts me, for whatever reason, mamatay ako, matanggal, oh ano sa buhay na ito. Sinabi ko sa inyo, isa sa mga opisyal, do not, do not abandon. Resolbahin ninyo ang problema na iyan kasi sisirain ang Pilipinas niyan." (If that problem outlasts me, for whatever reason, I died, I am removed from this life. I say to you, I said to one of your officers, do not, do not abandon it. Resolve this problem because this will destroy the Philippines.)

He ended his speech by extolling the troops to act on their own in this wise.

It is my opinion that if President Duterte will suddenly be gone, then the military will act on its own and take control of the government. (Atty. Al Vitangcol)

Yes, there are a lot of possibilities if worse comes to worst and we suddenly become a leaderless country. But for now let us give our support to President Duterte but be very vigilant and carry a lot of prayers in our heart that such eventuality will not happen because all of us will be dragged into the pits. Let's hope that will not be our destination. Sadly, it is now rumored that some of the people in the President's loop are not thinking the same and few were concerned about is "what's in it for me" coupled with arrogance. They should gather their act together and make his presidency lasts up to the last day.

ooO0Ooo

11.

China's 5th Column

Erick San Juan

Dateline, September 27, 2016

America's overall image around the world remains largely positive. Across the nations surveyed (excluding the U.S.), a median of 69% hold a favorable opinion of the U.S., while just 24% express an unfavorable view. However, there is significant variation among regions and countries.

In the aftermath of the Great Recession, many foreign commentators including Americans remarked that the era of U.S. dominance of the global economy and position as sole superpower were at an end. However, in the intervening years, a sustained economic recovery in the U.S. has bolstered its leadership credentials, and in the current survey, about twice as many people worldwide say that the U.S., and not China, is the world's leading economy.

Nonetheless, global public perception continue to express the view that China either has or eventually will replace the U.S. as the leading superpower. (Source Pew Research Center)

America's image is mostly positive among the Asian nations polled. Among these countries surveyed was the Philippines with an 85 percent score in 2014 and 92 percent in 2015 according to the Global Attitudes Project of Pew Research Center in Washington DC. People were asked "Do you have a favorable or unfavorable view of the US?"

Methinks we still maintain a high percentage score up to this moment with a favorable view of the US in spite of the 'bullish' attitude of our president towards some high-ranking American officials. Some observers believe that President Rody Duterte, in the midst of his balancing act between the US and China, is actually showing that he favors China more.

But the present administration has to be wary because the current war on drugs not only in and out of the largest prison camp like the National Bilibid Prison involves some confirmed Triad gang Chinese nationals. And the perennial problem in the South China Sea over territories that we won from the Hague's Permanent Court of Arbitration is not being recognized and respected by China, and in the process, our fishermen are still being 'harassed'.

The perception is that the US is still the better 'devil' that we know than the red Chinese who has exported their underworld ops to our country instead of being grateful to the Filipinos who gave them comfort several times and second home where they now become the 'novo' rich.

We have to be wary of China's sleepers (hybernated spies) and DPA (deep penetration agents) pretending to be part of the social media and our society. They are just waiting in the wings to take over anytime.

Remember the Japanese agents in the Philippines before the second world war. Most of them are lowly employees, drivers, gardeners, small time merchants, etc. but when the war erupted, they metamorphosed and our parents were shocked to know that their neighbor was a military officer of the Japanese Imperial Army.

It could be worst this time, these pro-Beijing ethnic chinese basically control everything. Many politicians, key government functionaries, even some officials in our AFP, PNP, judiciary and the 'church' are now in their pockets.

Be vigilant always. These sleepers are now bold enough to attack us. The mere fact that even their Facebook pages and social media accounts are fictitious.

And I got this message from a rich friend from China- "it's a pity that overseas Chinese especially in the Philippines taught that China can save them in a nuke war. We have more billionaires here in China not flaunting their wealth nor included at Forbes Magazine richest. If China's nuke hit the Philippines, they will be part of the so called collateral damage whether they like it or not."

Who do we believe now? Beware of the propaganda machines. The program is on.

Touche!

oo00o

12.

Live Bullet War Exercises, a Prelude to a Real War

Erick San Juan

(Dr. Erick San Juan is a political analyst, book author, writer, forum moderator, TV and radio broadcast commentator. He is a DOCTOR OF LETTERS. You can listen to his daily program thru DWSS 1894 khz AM at 5;30pm, under broadcast title, "Whistleblower.")

Dateline, September 19, 2016

The fifth annual China-Russia naval drill (that will go on for eight days) started last Monday, featuring stalwarts from both navies in action at the eastern waters of Zhanjiang, in Guangdong province, the HQ of the People's Liberation Army (PLA) Navy Nanhai Fleet.

Considering this is the first time that the Joint Sea is happening in the South China Sea, apocalyptic alarms from the usual suspects could not be more predictable – and thoroughly dismissed by the Beijing leadership. (Pepe Escobar @Reuters online)

Usually, the joint military exercise between Russia and China took place in the Sea of Japan also known as East Asia.

What a coincidence that a US military drill named 'Variant Shield', 2,000 miles to the east, the US military around the Pacific gathered for a two weeks drill with 18,000 personnel, 180 aircrafts and USS Ronald Reagan aircraft carrier.

Overheard that President Rody Duterte said that any possible miscalculation during such naval exercise in the contested area, using live ammunitions at that, might lead to a regional conflict. Ominous?

But can we blame President Duterte by thinking such possibility might happen? Actually there are other observers who feel the same and fear the same might just occur if either side will not be careful during the military exercises.

It is in this context that we should allow and continue our military relationship with the US, whether we like it or not, our status as a treaty ally of the US did not start last June 30, 2016. With the cooperation of our past leaders (others were collaborators) with Uncle Sam in the name of national security and to preserve democracy, various treaties were signed.

Revisiting some of these treaties by the present administration will somehow correct the lopsided parts where we are being shortchanged and the fact that such agreements should be ratified by the proper institutions like our Congress and not just the Executive branch.

Of course we welcome the statement of President Duterte of an independent foreign policy for the country but it should be handled with utmost diplomacy without hurting our existing allies for so many years now. And like any policy, it should be without bias and always for the common good and not only for the favored few. Pres. Duterte if he will do it right, can use this as a leverage and his charting an independent policy will be a good bargaining point with the Americans and with China. A balancing act that should be supported by the people.

In the course of the President's balancing act locally and globally, he should listen to the Filipino people who believe in him and in what he can do for the good of this nation if he doesn't want to be called a dictator in the making.

In his article, Duterte's 'shock and awe' diplomacy, La Salle professor Richard Javad Heydarian cited some of his observations on the President's kind of diplomacy and his attitude towards certain matters – "For those, who have underestimated his ability to reconfigure existing relations with the Southeast Asian country's most enduring ally, the United States, the past two weeks have been a rude awakening. Rapidly consolidating power over key institutions of the state, and backed up by robust support among various civil society groups, Duterte is in a position to redirect the Philippines' foreign policy like none of his predecessors."

"I'm really a rude person. I'm enjoying my last time as a rude person," Duterte famously promised earlier. "When I become president, when I take my oath of office . . . there will be a metamorphosis." It was a statement of re-assurance that compelled many to (mistakenly) presume that Duterte's tough campaign-period rhetoric – including those directed at America – was nothing but a clever gimmick.

So when Duterte embarked on his global diplomatic debut, attending the Association of Southeast Asian Nations (ASEAN) summit, many were expecting a more subdued and statesmanlike Duterte. Instead, the world witnessed a Hyde and Jekyll diplomatic behavior. Duterte, who accepted the Philippines' (rotational) chairmanship of the regional group, gracefully embraced his fellow Asian leaders, who appreciated his pragmatism on the South China Sea disputes and relations with China, while going on the offensive against the United States President Barack Obama, who was on his final official trip to Asia.

After uttering what appeared as expletives against the American president, the much-anticipated Obama-Duterte bilateral meeting was cancelled. Shortly after, amid growing panic over a potential diplomatic meltdown, Manila released a statement of "regret", while the Obama administration reiterated that U.S.-Philippine relations remain "rock solid." Duterte clarified that his foul-mouthed remarks weren't direct at Obama, who reassured his Filipino partners that he didn't take Duterte's insulting remarks personally.

Yet, just when everyone thought that the damage control efforts were bearing fruit, Duterte once again went on the offensive. And most recently has even asked, albeit rhetorically so far, American special forces in the troubled region of Mindanao to get out of the country. He has also made it clear that he is setting his sights on more robust ties, including military, with eastern powers of Russia and China. In fact, Duterte is expected to embark on his state visit to China, a first by any Filipino leader, in coming weeks. In a span of months, Philippine-US relations have gone from special and sacrosanct to uncertain and jittery. And this seems to be the new normal in one of the most intimate and enduring bilateral relations on the planet."

Are we going to end the most enduring bilateral relations that we had for years now and start a new bilateral relations with China?

Methinks it's better to deal with the 'devil' we know than a perceived 'angel' with the same clothes and interest like the demon. I hope Pres. Duterte will be in the right direction to correct our misfortunes.

Just asking.

ooOOoo

13.

Who's Fault: The Salesman or The Product?

Erick San Juan
Dateline, October 4, 2016

Another war is going on, aside from the war on drugs, it's coming from the very vocal supporters and non-supporters of President Rody Duterte. Strong words coming from both sides are everywhere – on the internet via the social media especially at the Facebook and Twitter, the texters who are very active giving their views even on radio and on television. And there are radio stations giving air time to callers airing their sentiments and can easily be recognized if one is for or against the present administration.

There is a growing number of Filipinos who are perceived gradually realizing that they voted a leader who is fast becoming an enemy, not only inside the country but even outside of this country but no matter what, the pro-Duterte will always fight to defend their leader up to the end.

Sadly the country is again divided, as if nobody is minding the store. Blunder after blunder, mistakes not checked by people in his loop before releasing information to the public. If only some key people in the Palace are responsible enough and did their homework, 'hindi malulubak ng madalas ang Pangulo'. Although there are several times that it's the President's fault when he made remarks against people or organization due to his heightened emotion based on past experiences. But if President Duterte is quick to make harsh comments, he is also quick to apologize if he believes he committed a mistake. But pundits believe that a leader should act and talk as real head of the state. Some concerned citizens on air requested the president not to talk like he owns the nation and drag everyone in a possible war which we will all regret. Another unsolicited advice on air this afternoon was about 'respect begets respect' and cussing and loose talk could backfire.

Close to his first 100 days in office, a lot of positive things happened especially on the war on drugs despite the expected jailing of big fishes, masterminds and financiers from the underworld. Everybody were shock to see thousands of users-pushers surrendered. But in the process he is now fighting several fronts as the growing number of pros and cons are in the 'blame game' mode.

So much can be seen of these pros and cons in front of national TV as the country's legislators are investigating the so-called extra-judicial killings in aid of legislation.

On the internet, several points were given in favor of the President. The Republic Defenders, a group of respected professionals commented that-

"In our 71 years of being independent, this is the first time we have a president who is not like the rest. He is genuinely pro-poor and was elected by the people without the support of traditional politicians and self serving businessmen. Some people are afraid that because of PRRD's political will and genuine desire to improve our country's plight, the oligarchs may be displaced. The traditional politicians' shenanigans may be uncovered. The narco generals and their lieutenants and the narco politicians may be unmasked. The gambling lords may lose their business. All of them run the risk of ending up in jail and/or losing their riches."

"These are the conditions that is why President Duterte is already fighting so many fronts, in various factions because he is very firm and sincere in his war on drugs and corruption that those who are hit, tends to retaliate by finding ways to topple him down or worst, assassinate him."

"PRRD is not the typical president who had to horse trade to win. Thus, he has a free hand to do as he deems best for the Philippines. This is the first time his supporters which run into the millions continue to involve themselves in the affairs of government and openly declare support for PRRD to the extent of using their own funds."

"His cabinet is composed mostly of septuagenarians, where money is no longer the main objective, but to leave legacies behind."

"He touched base with the poor specially the leftists such that for the first time, his SONA was not picketed but supported by the masses."

"PRRD is tough and walks his talk. He and his selected men cannot be bribed. Therefore, the crooked and the rich are no longer within their comfort zones."

The abovementioned are just some of the statements observed by those in favor of the leadership of the present administration.

On the contrary, the opposite are also aired through the internet by some factions who are not in favor of what the present leadership is doing and saying.

They see the push for an independent foreign policy of the government (but in favor of China and Russia) as an "attack on the west to appease the east" particularly the country's decades-long ties with the United States and our membership with the United Nations.

It is some kind of a suicidal move to break our tie with the US by putting an end to all military exercises and in the process scrapping bilateral military agreements.

Some anti-communist groups are more fiery in their attack against PRRD claiming that " if you quack like a duck, walk like a duck, you're a duck." They said that the people should not just be vigilant every time PRRD talks but be wary of his actions.

A former communist turned nationalist warned that a possible repeat of the Bolshevik revolution, a Stalin or Castro of Cuba takeover is in the offing.

A retired military officer disclosed that it could be a combination of all scenarios. He reminded discreetly some of his friends that it could be what they call in the intelligence lingo 'painting in the west but fighting in the east'. Meaning the possible air,sea and land battle between China and other country claimants at the South China Sea is not feasible due to so many allies war machines nearby.

But a purging from within is believed to be a possibility especially now that the PRRD administration has given the left an alliance which the left hardliners could fasttrack their real agenda. He added that since the AFP and the Department of Education scrapped the ROTC military training including the hibernated Congressional Committee Against Anti-Filipino Activities, it reportedly emboldened China to recruit young chinoys to be sleepers and trained PLA soldiers in disguise as taking their vacation in mainland China.

A scary scenario which happened in the past when the Japanese OFW's in the Philippines metamorphosed into officers of the Japanese Imperial Army when the war broke out.

The President's men were put on the spot on how and what to answer when asked if the government is really serious about his move without hurting our diplomatic ties with the US and PRRD's image in the international scene.

Really, a lot of balancing act like we are in a circus, and the Duterte administration is just beginning.

How far can the President's men and women go to defend his every word that is not music to a lot of ears, and how often they will say sorry to every mistake? And in the end, when worse comes to worst, who's fault? The salesman or the product?

14.

A Trump Presidency and the Consequences for Filipinos

Rodel Rodis

(Send comments to Rodel50@gmail.com or mail them to the Law Offices of Rodel Rodis at 2429 Ocean Avenue, San Francisco, CA 94127 or call 415.334.7800).

Dateline, Aug. 5, 2016, Inquirer.net, US Bureau

PH-US war games start amid uncertainty
Filipina in Florida charged in law professor's killing
Fil-Ams from Chicago, Florida, LA, DC among TOFA awardees
Traffic solutions sans emergency powers
Veteran broadcaster Nestor (Ness) Ocampo, 1941 – 2016

PH foreign policy to benefit China–Fitch
What's with end of Edca remark, asks military
US Supreme Court to hear Filipino's deportation case
Duterte, Hitler and the zeal to kill
Filipina teen activist is hailed as 'global innovator'

On the 74th anniversary of the bombing of Pearl Harbor, Republican presidential nominee Donald J. Trump dropped what the *London Daily Telegraph* called a "bombshell" when he announced that if elected president of the United States, he would implement a "total and complete shutdown of Muslims entering the United States."

Trump's campaign manager at the time Corey Lewandowski explained that Trump's proposed ban would apply to "everybody," including Muslims seeking immigrant visas as well as tourists seeking to enter the country. The ban would even apply to American Muslims who are currently overseas – presumably including members of the military and diplomatic service, another Trump staffer added.

Trump's proposed Muslim ban drew outrage from leaders in Asia who warned that Trump was helping the cause of ISIS by feeding Islamic State propaganda that depicted a grand war between Islam and the West.

"By uttering such a hate-spreading statement, Donald Trump has committed a crime by indirectly helping the cause of so-called global Islamist militants such as Islamic State," the chairman of the Jamiatul Ulama Bangladesh, an Islamic scholars council, told the press.

No PH reaction

But there was no outcry from Philippine officials or civil society that this bigoted policy would harm the 15 percent of the Philippine population that is Muslim. Were Filipino Christians willing to throw their Muslim brothers and sisters under the Trump bus?

Even the Filipino American community remained painfully silent on this issue. I confess that I too did not denounce Trump and his xenophobic bigotry in my columns published in the US and in the Philippines. I was content to just post my revulsion with Trump in my Facebook page.

In Indonesia, the world's most populous Muslim nation, Zuhairi Misrawi, an Islamic scholar from Muslim organization Nahdlatul Ulama, said the call was "a step backwards" for America. "We previously regarded America as a role model for democracy, equality, peace and justice," he said.

Trump's proposed Muslim ban relies on a US law that grants the president the authority to issue executive orders to prevent the entry of any class of people who would be considered "detrimental to the interests of the United States."

Detrimental to the interests of the United States? Sen. Lindsey Graham (R-South Carolina) pointed out that Trump's comments are "hurting the war effort and putting our diplomats and soldiers serving in the Middle East at risk. The way to win this war is to reach to the vast majority of people in Islamic faith who reject ISIS and provide them the capability to resist this ideology."

Perhaps in response to severe criticism from fellow Republicans about his religious intolerance, Trump modified his position so it would not expressly ban Muslims simply because of their faith. In his acceptance speech on July 21, Trump announced that he would now ban immigration from countries "compromised by terrorism."

Without mentioning the word "Muslim," Trump said: "We must immediately suspend immigration from any nation that has been compromised by terrorism until such time as proven vetting mechanisms have been put in place," Trump said. "We don't want them in our country."

When pressed by Meet the Press TV host Chuck Todd about whether his ban on immigration from countries "compromised by terrorism" would include countries like France and Belgium which have suffered terrorist attacks in recent years,

Trump declined to answer. Instead, he replied, "It's their own fault, because they've allowed people over years to come into their territory."

Guess which country in Southeast Asia has been most "compromised by terrorism"?

PH 'compromised by terrorism'?

Aside from Indonesia, with its Jamiyah Islamiyah militants, the Philippines would also be high on the list with its own homegrown terrorists, Abu Sayyaf, which is based in Sulu and Basilan in Mindanao. The Abus have waged a brutal campaign of bombings, kidnappings and assassinations, killing Filipinos and foreign nationals since their founding in 1991, as an offshoot of the Moro National Liberation Front. In 2004, they claimed responsibility for the bombing of Superferry 14 killing 116 people.

In 2014, the Abu Sayyaf, led by its leader, Isnilon Totoni Hapilon, pledged its loyalty to Abu Bakr al-Baghdadi, the leader of ISIS. Since then, it has been kidnapping foreigners for ransom and mercilessly beheading them if its demands are not met.

So if Trump is elected president, Philippine tourists may be barred from entering the US even for those with US relatives who are diehard Republicans who voted for Trump. Filipinos don't even have to be Muslim to be barred from entry as long as the Philippines is deemed a country "compromised by terrorism." The rest of the Philippines would now be included along with the 15 percent Muslim that would be thrown under the Trump bus. United at last.

As Trump would say, "It's their fault, they've allowed (Muslims) over the years to come into their territory." Of course, Muslims have lived in the Philippines since before the Spaniards came. In fact, Manila was a Muslim settlement under Rajah Soliman (Suleyman) when the Spaniards invaded it in 1565.

We can't ignore it now, can we?

Abu Sayyaf terrorist band. INQUIRER FILE

There is another Trump campaign promise that would also dramatically affect Filipinos. Trump has vowed to deport an estimated 11.3 million "illegal immigrants" in the US. Many believe the actual number to be much higher, at least 15 million. Although the emphasis in the media has focused mostly on Latinos who crossed the border from Mexico, the list includes probably 500,000 Filipinos, those affectionately called TNTs ("*tago nang tago*" – always hiding).

Trump would deport 500K Filipinos

Experts posit that it would take 20 years to remove "illegals" or "undocumented" aliens from the US, an estimate provided by the American Action Forum (AAF), a conservative think tank that released a 2015 study that showed that it would require 650 busloads every month for two decades. The total cost of a 20-year mass deportation program would be about $600 billion.

The AAF Report also conservatively estimated that "illegals" make up about 6.4 percent of the US labor force – about 11 million in 2014. Deporting them would shrink the US economy by nearly 6 percent or $1.6 trillion by 2035.

Many of the TNTs who would be deported by a President Trump have lived in the US for more than 20 years, are working in low-paying jobs, and regularly remit money to their relatives in the Philippines.

Of the $25 billion a year in overseas Filipino remittances to the Philippines, about 45 percent comes from the US and a large proportion of these funds comes from TNTs. Their deportation from the US would devastate the Philippine economy.

Filipino American voters in the November elections in the US should realize the political consequences of their vote.

(Send comments to Rodel50@gmail.com or mail them to the Law Offices of Rodel Rodis at 2429 Ocean Avenue, San Francisco, CA 94127 or call 415.334.7800).

ooo0Ooo

15.

The Spread of Child Trafficking

Fr. Shay Cullen
PREDA Foundation

Dateline, Sept. 19, 2016, Reflections

$32 BILLION IN PROFITS IS GENERATED BY THE HUMAN TRAFFICKING INDUSTRY EVERY YEAR

   Unpleasant as it is we must not turn the page, look away and ignore this social evil that is destroying the lives of hundreds of thousands of children and families. The spread of child sexual abuse all over the world is the terrible crime that few want to acknowledge and fight.

The high number of trafficked children, abducted and sold into the sex trade in developed and developing countries is unbelievable but at least 2.5 million are thought to be victimized at any given time and more are added to that list daily. The fact that so little is spent and done to combat it is an indictment of the international community and national government officials who tolerate it. Officials actually promote and license the establishments that foster sex tourism and human trafficking.

Hundreds of thousands of sex tourists from developed countries come to Southeast Asia every year to engage in pernicious acts of child sexual abuse and sex trafficking. The Philippines is notorious for these crimes of human trafficking and child abuse and many customers are coming from international pedophile rings. They abuse the children, make videos and sell them online. The international authorities do little to intervene and local authorities seem to condone and promote the trade in young people in the sex industry.

The institutional Catholic Church fails to challenge sufficiently this pernicious evil that destroys the fabric of family life. People of all beliefs and principles, social justice advocates and those who value human rights and dignity ought to be outraged and take action wherever they can. They can campaign with groups online and challenge their politicians to act to protect children and curb foreign aid to governments that fail to implement international child protection standards.

The human right workers, child protectors and the NGOs working to save, protect and heal the victims and bring abusers to justice are the wonder workers of the children who are rescued and saved. But they are underfunded, sidelined and most time ignored by the authorities who do not like their outspoken defense of the abused. The judicial system mostly fails them by dismissing the charges against their rapists and traffickers. At times bribery payments under and over the table allow the culprits to walk free of responsibility for their crimes.

Not only are the children hurt and damaged most beyond healing and recovery but families are destroyed by unfaithful husbands frequenting the sex bars and karaoke bars where young girls are offered to them. Some become addicted to this underage sex abuse and they can easily fall into incestuous relationships in their own families and abuse their own children. The spread of the underage sex business would account for the rapid increase in the incidents of incestuous abuse cases in the Catholic Philippines.

The foreign sex tourists become addicted also and then return to their own countries and will endanger children in their own families or communities. They will also participate in live cyber-sex events over the internet having made contacts with the sex bars and clubs making the evil shows of children doing sex acts on live internet connections. They send payments through international courier services and they can order up live shows to their own twisted lustful desires.

The most notorious of all in the Philippines is Australian pedophile and video maker Peter Scully.

He has been charged with 69 charges of criminal offenses of child abuse and making videos of him have brutal sex with six year olds and killing them on video. His production, "The Destruction of Daisy" shows many horrific crimes.

Dutch police discovered his video online. It was referred to the Australian Federal Police in Manila and the Philippine National Bureau of Investigation. They eventually caught Scully and his helpers. They were Local Filipino young women who recruited the children for him. The remains of "Daisy" was dug up in a house he rented. He is just one of perhaps hundreds doing this secret and hidden crime. How widespread it is, no one can say since it is illegal and done in secret.

The words condemning human trafficking and the sex trade in young people are in the millions. Human trafficking, cyber sex and sex tourism have all been decried, condemned and denounced. All lectures, interventions and hand-wringing seem to be of little or no purpose. The trade is growing and more children are falling into the grip of human traffickers, pimps and sex bar operators.

They have special impunity and enjoy police protection and government officials will issue the establishments with operating permits. They appear to be a legitimate business but behind the flashing neon lights and gaudy facades there is much exploitation.

The cyber-crime, where child sex is offered live on-line, is one of the most pernicious internet crimes and most difficult to investigate. It is a secret world where minors are raped and abused.

Pope Francis declared human trafficking of minors to be a modern form of slavery and a crime against humanity. We would all do good to take a stand in our hearts and minds and let it flow into action. We can work for justice of these vulnerable children. They are the most important in the Kingdom as the master has said.

shaycullen@preda.org

ooOOoo

16.

War-On-Drugs A Challenge to Catholic Faith

Fr. Shay Cullen
Reflections, PREDA Foundation

Dateline, October 4, 2016

The Catholic Church and that means not only the leadership but the People of God who believe in Jesus of Nazareth and his teaching on the sacredness of life, mercy, compassion and understanding are challenged in this day by the War-on-Drugs. God's people in the Church needs to take a stand with, and reach out to those in need of healing, care and help. Drug dependents are the victim attacked by bandits and was cared for by the Good Samaritan on the road to Jericho.

The Philippine Church and everyone who considers him or herself a Catholic is challenged the commitment and fiery words of President Duterte to continue his war-on-drugs and remove as many suspects as possible.

Few can doubt the dedication and commitment to rid the Philippines of the drug menace. According to a United Nations report the Philippines has one of the highest uses of illegal drugs in Asia. Philippine Dangerous Board estimated statistics there are 1.8 million drug dependents in the Philippines,

The true Christian believers in Jesus of Nazareth and his teaching of justice, mercy, repentance and forgiveness with penance must think about the moral issues of this campaign and its methods of killing the suspects without evidence or trial is a big challenge to the Catholic Church. It is a call on the conscience and the integrity of the institutional leaders and The People of God everywhere and especially in Asia and the Philippines to take a stand on this.

Eighty percent of the population can be said to be Catholic and perhaps 60 percent know and believe in the commandment, "Thou shall not kill." They believe they must act and speak to protect life, practice love and mercy, to heal the wounded, has compassion, justice and forgiveness. Do unto others as you would want them to do unto you is at he hear of the message. Jesus in Matthew 25 said will be judged by the love and compassion we show to the hungry thirsty, naked, homeless and those we visit in jail. What we do to them we do to Jesus of Nazareth.

In a July 2016 poll by Pulse Asia a stunning 91% Filipinos said that they trusted in the president. The survey released on Wednesday, July 20 asked 1,200 Filipinos if they trusted in President Duterte and almost all answered yes. It was less than half a percent that said they did not trust him while less than half a percent distrusted him, and 8% were undecided.

Catholics are committed by their faith to uphold life, life in the womb of the unborn, life of the poor and the hungry, life of the oppressed and downtrodden and to take a stand for them. So the teaching of Jesus challenges them and the church to question the methods used in the war –on-drugs.

Those methods according to some commentators violate human rights and the dignity of the human person. Catholic faith if it is truly correct faith and not merely attending routinely Holy Mass, religious rites and rituals and singing hymns has to be seen flowing into action. St.James has said in his New Testament letter"Faith without good deeds is dead." Catholics are called by their faith to take a stand on the moral issue of justice and due process and the rights of the people to live and not be shot dead on the mere suspicion of a policeman who has sworn to protect the people not shoot them.

It true that catholic population is accepting it?

That is until it turns on their children and their relatives and they will feel that there is no church or civil institution left to protect their rights.

The Catholic Church has made a statement on the killing of suspects recently. The head of the catholic Bishops `conference of the Philippines (CBCP) Archbishop Soc Villegas signed a statement that deplored the violence.

"Although death is a twin sister born with us on the same day we were born, death by terror and violence, death in the hands of our fellowmen is a sin that cries to heaven for vengeance. With willful murder, we also grieve the sins of sexual perversion, oppression of the poor and the defrauding of laborers of their wages. Like murder, these sins cry to heaven for divine justice. We are not numb to these other offenses against human life".

Earlier, Manila Auxiliary Bishop Broderick Pabillo, De La Salle Philippines president Brother Jose Mari Jimenez, Ateneo de Manila University president Father Jose Ramon Villarin, and the Association of Major Religious Superiors of Women in the Philippines, among others, took turns in slamming the recent killings.

Novaliches Bishop Emeritus Teodoro Bacani appealed to the conscience of the authorities and other individuals to refrain from killing drug suspects.

It is the silence of the People of God in the Philippines to act on their belief in the sanctity of human life, the rule of law, the principal of "innocent until proven guilty."

Taking a stand and speaking out for justice, for what is just and right, what is true and good is what Catholic faith is all about and that is the challenge to the catholic communities everywhere.

shaycullen@preda.org

ooOOoo

17.

A Christmas Letter
to a Muslim
(a piece of nostalgic history)

Fred Natividad
Livonia, Michigan

(This letter was originally an email to a Turkish Muslim email pal after he shared his own story of Ramadan. Fred Natividad Posting from historic Virginia =Say nanlapuan lingawen pian antay arapen. =Alamin ang pinang-galingan upang malaman ang paro-roonan. = Know where we had been to guide us where we are going.)

Dateline, 2016

Deniz,
This is about Christmas in the Philippines. It is not quite like your Ramadan but both have religious overtones. Please note that I immigrated from the Philippines some four decades ago as of

this writing and cultural changes may have happened since then.

When we talk about Christmas in the Philippines let's start with the trite Philippine boast that it is predominantly a Catholic country. Filipino Catholics, the good and the bad, are proud of their Catholicism, a curious phenomenon considering that Catholicism was rammed down their throats with the point of a sword which began in 1521 when Ferdinand Magellan, on his way to the Spice Islands in Indonesia, stumbled into what is now the Philippines.

Christmas traditions, therefore, evolved from what Spanish friars taught Filipinos for 377 years from 1521 to 1898.

Today, many Catholic Filipinos among the supposedly sophisticated, crassly materialistic crowd, dutifully go to communion, contribute generously to the collection box, or belong to supposedly pious Catholic groups. Hypocrisy is blatantly transparent among them. But that's another story, best left for explanation to experts in human religious behavior who might be able for instance to shed light on why, at a supposedly subdued religious celebration to honor the Virgin Mary, various devotee groups compete with arrogant vanity as to who has the best looking and most expensively attired statuette of the Virgin Mary.

To a non-Filipino observer the parade of several statuettes of the Virgin Mary during a procession amidst a mechanical recitation of 10 Our Fathers, 50 Hail Marys and a host of mumbled songs would seem like a sarcastic, comical parody of whatever piety the friars taught early Filipinos.

My wife has her own way of piety.She secludes herself to a corner of our darkened bedroom and does quietly her 10 Our Fathers and 50 Hail Marys, oblivious to my screams over the blaring TV when the Chicago Bears get a touchdown.

Anyway, back to Christmas that I remember.

Each year, beginning on the 16th of December, dawn masses are held daily. The last one will be the midnight mass on the 24th - a total of nine days of prayers (novena). Luckily there is no such thing as snow in the Philippines to bog down oxcarts. In lieu of snow tropical rains are equally a nuisance but Decembers are blissfully drier and pleasant. Oxcarts, by the way, had become extinct, replaced by a unique contraption called jeepneys.

A jeepney, by the way, evolved from surplus jeeps left by the US military in the last war. They were converted into minibusses and redecorated with garish "artwork." They became the ubiquitous mode of public transportation.

In the old days nine-day Christmas services were held in the mornings supposedly ordered by friars. Peasants who compose the majority population of the country played hooky if they can get away with it because they had to work on their fields early in the mornings before the tropical sun would make working in the fields intolerable.

Spanish authorities - there was no separation of church and state for three and a half centuries - decided to order masses be held at dawn so the peasants would have no more excuses in missing morning services. Dawns in December, however, are still dark because the

Philippines, though in the tropics just above the equator, are in the northern hemisphere.

Grumbling peasants therefore trudged to church while it is still "night," hence they called a dawn service "simbang gabi," or "night mass." Aside from losing some sleep they had to listen to the hated friars recite some Latin stuff they don't understand, on top of which they, the impoverished peasants had to plunk down some precious coins into the collection basket. They support the comfortable life of the friars.

The dawn masses eventually became treasured traditions and to some extent had assumed some social facades, where one can optionally choose to preen while pretending to pray. Recalling my childhood Christmases, the tradition of receiving gifts (or scheming to receive gifts) were not limited on Christmas Day itself. If we missed receiving a gift on Christmas Day from a favorite uncle or aunt or from a baptismal godfather or godmother it was all right to ambush him or her any day thereafter until January 6 of the new year.

Filipinos are not just pious - they are also superstitious. If the three kings gave gifts to The Baby on January 6, then it must be all right for Philippine uncles, aunts, and godparents to dole out Christmas gifts up to that date, too!

In other words, the Christmas season in the Philippines runs from December 16 to January 6, a total of 22 days! For 22 evenings children will go all over the neighborhood serenading houses with Christmas carols. No matter how much they murdered "Silent Night" or "Jingle Bells" with their out of tune vocal chords and mispronounced

English words they will be rewarded with a few coins.

As early as November some houses would already sport bamboo-ribbed paper star lanterns hanging on windows, obviously a practice inspired by the bright star over Bethlehem when Jesus was born. Today, high tech lights lacing neighborhood windows supplement the paper lanterns. Making giant paper lanterns has evolved into a fascinating art, especially in a province called Pampanga, in the vicinity of what used to be the largest overseas American air force base. The lanterns are not only huge but are also intricately designed with multicolored blinking electric bulbs. They have to be seen to be appreciated.

The base, by the way, is gone because Philippine leaders, in their infinite wisdom, refused to renew the 99-year old lease of the huge airfield. Anyway the base was destroyed by the deadly eruption of Mt. Pinatubo.

The Spanish friars taught Filipinos to honor saints with celebrations called "fiestas." Traditionally, during a fiesta, any stranger can come to any house and partake of holiday food. Fiestas are therefore expensive and financially draining but Filipinos, poor as they are, learned to love these fiestas which became their chance to show how hospitable they can be in spite of their miserable poverty stricken lives.

The Christmas midnight mass has become one such fiesta. Young men would escort their girlfriends to church. After the mass they would proceed to the house of any friend who invited them or to their own houses or their girlfriends' for the traditional gluttony that will last into the wee hours of dawn. One favorite repast will be hot, thick, rice soup with huge chunks of chicken (arroz caldo con pollo in Spanish). There may be all sorts of rice cakes and sugared ginger tea. Or there may be hot chocolate drink made from scratch. Cacao beans from a backyard are dried, roasted, ground, sugared and molded into the native version of an American Hershey bar and then melted in boiling water to become hot chocolate drink...

Today, in homes made more affluent by dollar laden balikbayans (vacationing overseas foreign workers), there will be expensive Scotch whiskey, ham, sweet meats, imported oranges, grapes...

It came to pass that after three and a half centuries, in 1898, Filipinos finally kicked the Spaniards out, looking to Americans as allies because the Spanish-American war broke out. When the USS Maine exploded in far away Cuba this American admiral named Dewey was "coincidentally" in Hongkong with his complement of modern, deadly US navy ships. He steamed into Manila Bay and, without a single casualty, leisurely destroyed the decrepit Spanish fleet. Filipinos were jubilant until they realized that historic naval Battle of Manila Bay Dewey had no intention to sail back to San Francisco.

Sometime earlier a prescient character named Jose Rizal intelligently analyzed events that were current at the time. He brought out the possibility that within a century the "great north American republic" (his words translated from Spanish) would get involved in the Philippines. In 1896 the Spaniards executed him by firing squad for his nationalism. A couple of years later the

Americans, paved by Dewey and the United States Navy, did come to occupy the Philippines.

Rizal was right.

By the way, Jose Rizal studied medicine. He chose ophthalmology as his specialty so he can treat his mother's failing eyesight. He came the Philippine national hero because he was also an ardent nationalist. Among a host of other talents, was a writer, a sculptor, and a poet. He had a penchant for studying international languages. Aside from Spanish, his main vehicle in his writings, he also learned English, Japanese, German, etc. - about 22 foreign languages in all at a time when the world was not yet a technological global village.

He was also reputed to be a ladies man in his international travels. Although his true love was his distant cousin he wound up living with an Irish girl half his age.

Back to Christmas in the Philippines...

The American invasion started the gradual, heavy Hollywoodization of the Philippines. One result of that cultural morphing is that some features of the Philippine Christmas season are ridiculous. Cold country motifs, no matter how blatantly out of character in the torrid tropics, will dominate the season's ambience. There will be pine trees decorated with artificial snow! At Christmas parties and at stores there will be heavily costumed Santa Clauses sweltering in the ninety degree heat. There will be a sprinkling of native ditties in the air but what will predominate wafting all over the archipelago of at least 7,100 islands will be the classic strains of Irving Berlin's

"White Christmas," and other American Christmas favorites like Jingle Bells and Silent night…

But, hey, Christmas is Christmas in whatever way or form. So, as they say in the Philippines, "Maligayang Pasko!"

You can guess what that means…

oo0Ooo

18.

Philippine President Rodrigo Duterte Gives the EU the Finger

John Ciorciari
Associate Professor of Public Policy,
University of Michigan

Courtesy of visayans@yahoogroups.com
Dateline, October 6, 2016 8:21 PM

(Disclosure Statement.
John Ciorciari does not work for, consult, own
shares in or receive funding from any company or
organization that would benefit from this article,
and has disclosed no relevant affiliations beyond
the academic appointment above. Partners
University of Michigan provides funding as a
founding partner of The Conversation US. View all
partners. Republish this article. We believe in the
free flow of information. We use a Creative
Commons Attribution No Derivatives licence, so
you can republish our articles for free, online or in
print. Republish Philippine President Rodrigo
Duterte gives the EU the finger on Sept. 20, 2016.
REUTERS/Lean Daval Jr.
- Email - Twitter47 - Facebook147 - LinkedIn - Print)

U.S. efforts to promote peace and stability in the South China Sea are facing a new challenge. This time, the difficulty comes not from China but from the leader of a U.S. treaty ally – President Rodrigo Duterte of the Philippines. In recent weeks, the U.S.-Philippine alliance has come under strain as Duterte has rebuked the United States and threatened drastic changes in Philippine foreign policy. His volatile behavior threatens the alliance, President Obama's strategy for "rebalancing" to Asia and the stability of the Southeast Asian strategic landscape.How is incendiary rhetoric like Duterte's likely to affect a strong defense partnership and regional security more broadly? This is the kind of question my research on the international relations of the Asia-Pacific addresses.

Duterte's outbursts

Since taking office in late June, Duterte has launched a ruthless domestic war on drugs and declared that he doesn't "care about human rights." Those critical of his policies have met with his sharp, uninhibited tongue. "F-ck you," he most recently told his critics in the European Union. Senior officials from the United States, a treaty ally since 1951, have not been spared. Even mild U.S. criticism has irritated Duterte's thin skin, prompting him to describe U.S. Secretary of State John Kerry as "crazy" and call President Barack Obama a "son of a whore."

He has chided the United States as a former colonial power, announced plans to expel U.S. special forces engaged in counter terrorism training, halted joint patrols in the South China Sea and said he would consider buying arms from China and Russia. The line between Duterte's bombast and real policy views is unclear. He has already backtracked from his pledge to expel U.S. special forces and said the Philippines needs the United States in the South China Sea. Still, his volatility threatens the U.S.-Philippine alliance, the strongest check against unilateral Chinese expansion in the South China Sea.

Reorienting the Philippines?

Duterte's pledge to recalibrate Philippine foreign policy is not surprising. Under his predecessor Benigno Aquino, the feud between China and the Philippines in the South China Sea intensified. Both states prize the sea's hydrocarbon deposits, large fisheries and vital shipping lanes. The dispute over sovereignty also activates nationalist sentiment, as Cornell professor Jessica Chen Weiss and I stress in recent research.

China's launch of an island-building campaign in the South China Sea added fuel to the fire.As tension in the South China Sea rose, the U.S.-Philippine alliance strengthened to a level not seen since the Cold War. Arms sales, joint exercises and training increased, and a 2014 agreement gave U.S. troops extended access to Philippine military facilities. Not all Filipinos approved. Some derided the added U.S. military presence as an affront to sovereignty that would alienate Beijing without providing effective protection.

As I argued in my book "The Limits of Alignment," fears of losing autonomy and antagonizing foreign rivals are the most common reasons why Southeast Asian governments seek to limit their strategic relationships with great powers like China and the United States. Some analysts thus welcomed early indications that Duterte would pursue more "balanced relations" with China and the United States.

What has alarmed diplomats and strategists is the bold, inconsistent and temperamental nature of Duterte's foreign policy pronouncements. At times his reputation for impulsive speech is helpful diplomatically. It enables embarrassed Philippine officials and nervous international partners to downplay his remarks as hyperbole, as his aides did after he threatened to withdraw from the United Nations in August. Still, his comments have to be taken seriously.

Many observers discounted Duterte's campaign promises to employ brutal anti-drug tactics. With more than 3,500 suspected drug dealers killed since the start of July, his remarks were clearly more than electoral bluster.Discord between Duterte's rhetoric and the views of the security establishment add further uncertainty. In mid-September, as Duterte railed against American colonial abuses, the head of the Philippine armed services insisted that the alliance is "rock solid."

The possibility of abrupt moves or domestic fracture in the Philippines raise real dangers to regional stability.As Defense Secretary Ash Carter has stressed, a strengthened U.S.-Philippine alliance is a key to U.S. engagement in Southeast Asia. It represents a means for projecting American force and maintaining a larger regional presence over time. Just as importantly, it is a vehicle for demonstrating U.S. credibility and commitment to the region as China's waxing power and assertiveness test U.S. resolve.

Duterte's threats to expel U.S. special forces, cease joint patrols, and buy arms from China greatly complicate the implementation of the 2014 U.S.-Philippine defense agreement. The

United States does have other means to maintain a strong naval presence in Southeast Asia if cooperation stalls. For example, the U.S. regularly rotates naval warships through Singapore. But the United States has a clear disinterest in seeing one of its oldest Asian allies turn down American military protection in favor of direct talks with Beijing over the South China Sea. As a result, U.S. officials have been loath to criticize Duterte's domestic abuses or foreign policy plans too sharply.

Chinese responses

For its part, the Chinese government has welcomed Duterte's pronouncements cautiously. In state-owned media, Chinese analysts initially lauded Duterte's plans to abandon Aquino's "lopsided" and "unscrupulous" China policy but later remarked on his "reckless comments" and the Philippines' "uncertain future" under his leadership.

A September meeting between Duterte and Chinese premier Li Keqiang yielded cordial pledges to pursue better ties, but a breakthrough was not clearly in sight. Chinese officials seem to recognize that volatile leaders can swing in more than one direction. Moreover, anti-China nationalist sentiment is widespread in the Philippines and among the military leadership, constraining Duterte's ability to compromise. His high approval ratings – 91 percent at the end of July – do not ensure that his harsh domestic policies or swings in foreign policy will not come back to haunt him.

Regional repercussions

Despite Duterte's domestic constraints, his embrace of bilateral talks is a boon for Beijing. China prefers to deal with smaller rival claimants over the South China Sea one by one. By contrast, the Philippines, Vietnam and several other Southeast Asian states have tried to "internationalize" the South China Sea dispute by involving the United States and "multilateralize" it by discussing it in regional forums where weaker states can pool their weight. Vietnam will suffer if Duterte spurns the United States and bypasses multilateral talks. Vietnam needs a strong U.S. security presence as a counterweight to China. However, the ideological gap and legacy of mistrust between Hanoi and Washington prevent Vietnam from hosting robust U.S. forces itself. If the Philippine-U. S. alliance weakens, Vietnam will have little choice but to adopt a more accommodating posture toward Beijing.

The Association of Southeast Asian Nations and its members will also suffer indirectly as Duterte's shift undermines efforts to manage the South China Sea issue multilaterally. These currents will be difficult to reverse.The adverse consequences of Duterte's approach may be greatest in the Philippines. With weak independent naval capacity and growing economic dependency on China, Philippine leverage in the South China Sea talks is limited. Concessions could prove explosive domestically.

Should Duterte alienate the United States and embrace China, he may well arouse domestic pressure to take a hard line toward Beijing without the means to enforce one – a dangerous position at home and abroad. While Duterte has planted the seeds of instability, he need not let them grow. The U.S. government and other Philippine partners will likely be willing to treat his recent remarks as products of a bad temper and a populist political campaign. That gives Duterte a second chance to expound a more calculated, pragmatic and well-scripted foreign policy.

-ooOOoo-

Why I Publish and/or Reprint Books And Why My Service is Free?

By Tatay Jobo Elizes, Self-Publisher

Writings are timeless and they act as mirrors of history. I publish writings as they remain relevant anytime. There are also writers who write a lot but never publish them. There are also old books with no more prints available. The solution is to publish/reprint.

I am offering these services free of charge because of the availability of print-books-on-demand (POD) system nowadays. I can produce the book, but the prints are not free. It's free because I want to encourage writing and reading to all.

Why put your writings in a book? And not just in the internet? I recommend that writings be retained in a hard copy or in book form or printed form for posterity. The book will always be there among your collections or libraries. Not all use the internet. The internet access has its technical problems. Writings in the internet may be erased erroneously. Free storage is hard to access. Paid storage may be returned or lost.

For those looking for a publisher, especially if you have a novel or many essays, I can produce the paperback book under your own authorship at no cost. I can produce art books, family tree books, family albums/pictorials, biographies, joke books, song hits books, travelogues, reunions, color or black & white, etc.

Please buy online as paperback or kindle at **http://tinyurl.com/mj76ccq** (copy and paste to your browser). Permission had been granted by the author/ authors to print their books under my free self-publishing service. They own copyrights to their works. Interested reader may request free reading of any of my books, articles or essays via online reading or ebook. Just email me: **job_elizes@yahoo.com** My Books Catalog can be seen at **www.jobelizes6.wix.com/mysite**. The catalogue will grow as years pass by because of additional titles to be published. I continue to publish or reprint books as a means to archive them in hard copy and/or digital form, for posterity and legacy. Thank you.

oo0Ooo